AZUSA PACIFIC UNIVERSITY

THE COGNITIVE PROFILES OF TWICE-EXCEPTIONAL
CHILDREN AND ADOLESCENTS

by

Laura McDonald

A dissertation submitted to the

School of Behavioral and Applied Sciences

in partial fulfillment of the requirements

for the degree Doctor of Psychology

Azusa, California

July, 2011

UMI Number: 3467980

All rights reserved

INFORMATION TO ALL USERS
The quality of this reproduction is dependent upon the quality of the copy submitted.

In the unlikely event that the author did not send a complete manuscript
and there are missing pages, these will be noted. Also, if material had to be removed,
a note will indicate the deletion.

UMI 3467980
Copyright 2011 by ProQuest LLC.
All rights reserved. This edition of the work is protected against
unauthorized copying under Title 17, United States Code.

ProQuest LLC
789 East Eisenhower Parkway
P.O. Box 1346
Ann Arbor, MI 48106-1346

AZUSA PACIFIC UNIVERSITY

THE COGNITIVE PROFILES OF TWICE-EXCEPTIONAL CHILDREN AND ADOLESCENTS

by

Laura McDonald

has been approved by the

School of Behavioral and Applied Sciences

in partial fulfillment of the requirements

for the degree Doctor of Psychology

Beth Houskamp, Ph.D., Committee Chair

Sheryn Scott, Ph.D., Committee Member

Robert Welsh, Ph.D., Committee Member

Rose Liegler, Ph.D., Interim Dean, School of Behavioral and Applied Sciences

© Copyright by Laura McDonald 2011

All Rights Reserved

DEDICATION

I wish to dedicate this dissertation to my husband and best friend, Brian. I cannot thank you enough for your support throughout graduate school and this dissertation process. Your love and support show no limit. I will be forever grateful for the sacrifices you have made to help me accomplish my goals and for your dedication to my dreams. I truly could not have done it without you. I love you more than words can express.

ACKNOWLEDGMENTS

This dissertation would not have been possible without the support, encouragement, and generosity of many. I would like to thank my outstanding dissertation committee, Dr. Beth Houskamp, Dr. Bob Welsh, and Dr. Sheryn Scott, for your excellent mentorship, guidance, support, and expertise. I am truly grateful to my chair, Dr. Beth Houskamp; you are not only a mentor, but have also become a true friend. You have been an inspiration to me, both professionally and personally. Your leadership, guidance, wisdom, kindness, and friendship are truly felt. Your passion for clinical work and research continues to inspire and motivate me. You have been more caring and encouraging than you will ever know. Dr. Bob Welsh, thank you for sharing my enthusiasm in research and statistics. Thank you for your statistical wisdom and for encouraging and supporting me in exploring unfamiliar statistical territory. Dr. Sheryn Scott, thank you for your enthusiasm, your tremendous clinical knowledge, and your many affirming words over the course of this project.

Thank you to Dr. Paul Beljan and Dr. Janiece Turnbull, the pediatric neuropsychologists who provided guidance and expertise. This study could not have been completed without your support.

To my parents, Stefan and Christa Hoch, thank you so much for your love and never-ending support. Thank you for always encouraging me to follow my dreams. You believed in me even when I did not believe in myself. *This* dream would not have been possible without your constant encouragement and generosity. To my sister, Julia, thank you for always being there for me and believing in me. You are the most amazing sister I could have asked for, and you will always be my close friend.

Finally, thank you to Marlon and Sienna. Thank you for the joy you bring to my life every single day. Your smiles, laughs, and hugs make everything worthwhile. I feel truly blessed to be your mom.

ABSTRACT

THE COGNITIVE PROFILES OF TWICE-EXCEPTIONAL
CHILDREN AND ADOLESCENTS

Laura McDonald
Doctor of Psychology, 2011
Azusa Pacific University
Advisor: Beth Houskamp, Ph.D.

Twice-exceptionality can be defined as the co-occurrence of intellectual giftedness and disability, including academic, social-emotional, and behavioral problems. There is a lack of empirical research examining the area of twice-exceptionality; and, as a result, there is insufficient support for the current definitions, identification criteria, and interventions employed for twice-exceptional individuals. The heterogeneity of this population highlights the importance of exploring the cognitive patterns present among twice-exceptional individuals to facilitate the identification as well as the treatment of this population. The present study examined the Wechsler Intelligence Scale, Fourth Edition (WISC-IV; Wechsler, 2003) profiles of 95 twice-exceptional children and adolescents to facilitate the discovery of subtype patterns present among this group. A two-stage cluster analysis revealed 7 twice-exceptional subtypes that were differentiated primarily by level of performance on the 4 factor scores. The identified twice-exceptional subtypes provide information about characteristic strengths and weaknesses that not only facilitate the identification of twice-exceptional students, but also carry implications for educational intervention.

TABLE OF CONTENTS

Dedication iii

Acknowledgments iv

Abstract vi

List of Tables xi

List of Figures xi

Chapter   Page

1. Introduction of the Literature 1

    Twice-Exceptionality 1

    Cognitive Abilities 5

    Problem Statement 8

2. Review of the Literature 10

    Giftedness 10

    Theories of Development 12

        Dabrowski's Theory of Positive Disintegration 12

        Silverman's Theory of Asynchronous Development 14

    Twice-Exceptionality 16

    Areas of Deficits: Learning Problems, Behavior Problems, and

        Social-Emotional Difficulties 19

        Learning Problems 19

Chapter	Page
Behavior Problems	25
Social-Emotional Difficulties	27
Misdiagnosis	29

  Identification 31

    Identification of Giftedness 31

    Identification of Twice-Exceptionality...34

    Identification of Gifted Students with Learning Disabilities...................36

    Identification of Gifted Students with Behavior or Emotional

        Problems 38

  Educational Needs 40

  Cognitive Abilities...42

    Wechsler Intelligence Scale for Children 42

    Wechsler Intelligence Scale for Children, Third Edition (WISC-III) 46

    Wechsler Intelligence Scale for Children, Fourth Edition (WISC-IV) 53

  Analysis of Cognitive Abilities 58

    Verbal Performance IQ Discrepancy 61

    Analysis of WISC Factors and Subtests..63

    Normative Profile Analysis 71

    Cluster Analysis...73

  Conclusion 78

3. Methods 81

  Participants 81

  Procedures 81

Chapter	Page
Measures	82
Data Analysis	84
4. Results	86
Descriptive Sample Statistics	87
Identification and Validation of a WISC-IV Typology	88
5. Discussion	103
Cluster Subtypes	107
Cluster 1	107
Cluster 2	110
Cluster 3	113
Cluster 4	115
Cluster 5	116
Cluster 6	119
Cluster 7	123
Cluster Validation	127
Clinical Implications	128
Educational Implications	132
Limitations	136
Future Research	137
References	139

Appendix	Page
A: Manuscript	152
B: Curriculum Vitae	193

LIST OF TABLES

Table 1: WISC-IV Full Scale IQ, Factor Index, and Subtest Scores for the
Entire Sample ($N = 95$)..88

Table 2: Mean Full Scale and Factor Index Scores and Standard Deviations
for the Seven Cluster Subtypes..90

Table 3: Mean Subtest Scores and Standard Deviations for the Seven Cluster
Subtypes..92

Table 4: Frequency of Gender and Ethnicity (Percentage) for the Seven WISC-IV
Cluster Subtypes 93

Table 5: Mean Ages and Ranges in Years for Each Cluster 93

Table 6: Primary Diagnoses (Count and Percentage) of the Seven Clusters....................95

Table 7: Secondary Diagnoses (Count and Percentage) of the Seven Clusters................95

LIST OF FIGURES

Figure 1: WISC-IV Factor Index Score Profiles for the Seven WISC-IV Cluster
Subtypes..90

CHAPTER 1

INTRODUCTION OF THE LITERATURE

Twice-exceptionality can be defined as the co-occurrence of intellectual giftedness and disability, including academic, social-emotional, and behavioral problems. Twice-exceptional children and adolescents are intellectually gifted, but they also experience disabilities such as learning difficulties, attention problems, depression, acting-out behaviors, or social awkwardness. There is a lack of empirical research examining the area of twice-exceptionality; and, as a result, there is insufficient support for the current definitions, identification criteria, and interventions employed for twice-exceptional individuals. The heterogeneity of this population indicates the importance of exploring the cognitive patterns present among twice-exceptional individuals to facilitate the identification as well as the treatment of this population. An exploration of the cognitive ability of twice-exceptional students may contribute to the understanding of this group by providing information about the strengths and weaknesses of this population. This will not only facilitate the identification and reduce misdiagnosis of twice-exceptional students, but also improve services for this underserved group.

Twice-Exceptionality

Children and adolescents who exhibit intellectual giftedness in conjunction with learning, social-emotional, or behavioral disabilities are referred to as twice-exceptional. These individuals demonstrate characteristics of two exceptionalities: intellectual gifts, as well as difficulties such as learning and attention deficits, depression, anxiety, anger, or acting out behaviors (National Association for Gifted Children [NAGC], 1998). However, gifts and deficits are typically viewed as being at opposite ends of a spectrum; and the concept of a gifted individual with a disability is often viewed as an oxymoron (Seeley, 1998). This is largely due to Terman's (1925) description of gifted students as being better in physical stature, having greater personal adjustment and emotional stability, being personally successful, having superior mental characteristics, having below-average incidence of suicide and mental illness, being more trustworthy and less likely to cheat, and having social attitudes that are more wholesome than the average person. This description led to the popular belief that gifted students are superior in many ways to the average population and contributed to the belief that giftedness and deficits cannot coexist in the same person.

Two theories addressing the development of gifted children and adolescents have provided a framework for understanding the areas of difficulty present among twice-exceptional individuals. These theories include Dabrowski's Theory of Positive Disintegration and Silverman's Theory of Asynchronous Development. Dabrowski (1964) described the emotional development of gifted individuals and suggested that these individuals experience psychomotor, sensual, intellectual, imaginational, and emotional realms with heightened intensity and complexity. Silverman (1997) used the term *asynchronous development* to describe giftedness as being out of sync with oneself, both internally and externally that can lead to inner tension and manifest itself in a great amount of scatter on IQ subtest scores (Webb et al., 2005).

Twice-exceptional children and adolescents may experience difficulty in the areas of learning, attention, behavior and social-emotional functioning. Learning problems most commonly include Reading Disorder, Mathematics Disorder, and Disorder of Written Expression, as well as nonverbal learning disabilities such as Attention Difficulties, Executive Functioning Deficits, and Auditory Processing Deficit. Behavior problems experienced by twice-exceptional individuals may include power struggles, arguments, temper tantrums, acting out, or sibling rivalry. These students may carry various diagnoses such as Oppositional Defiant Disorder, Conduct Disorder, Intermittent Explosive Disorder, or Disruptive Behavior Disorder NOS. Social-emotional problems such as anxiety, depression, or poor social relationships are further difficulties commonly experienced by twice-exceptional children and adolescents. There is a risk for the difficulties of these individuals to become the sole focus of interventions, while their giftedness remains unrecognized. As a result, misdiagnosis, misidentification or over-identification of diagnoses among twice-exceptional children unfortunately occur frequently (Webb et al., 2005). Additional research exploring the co-occurrence of giftedness and learning, behavior, and social difficulties is needed to facilitate the recognition and reduce misdiagnosis among this group.

Further complicating the identification of twice-exceptional children and adolescents is the fact that gifts and deficits frequently mask each other. For example, students may be identified as gifted; but their learning, behavior, or social-emotional deficits may be overlooked because their talents may compensate for their areas of difficulty. Other students may be identified as learning disabled or as suffering from a behavioral or social-emotional disability, while their giftedness remains unrecognized. A third group includes students whose gifts and deficits hide each other; and, therefore, both remain unrecognized. In addition, research investigating the area of twice-exceptionality is limited and relies largely on case studies, observations, and self-reports rather than empirical studies (Cohen & Vaughn, 1994). Moreover, research on twice-exceptionality has largely focused on gifted students with learning disabilities, while the co-occurrence of giftedness with behavior or social-emotional difficulties has been mostly neglected by previous research. As a result, there is a lack of knowledge regarding the characteristics of the twice-exceptional population; and research investigating this area is needed to aid in understanding this population and to provide clearer identification criteria and suitable intervention strategies for this understudied group.

While the use of intelligence tests has been viewed as the gold standard for the identification of giftedness, a number of barriers impede the identification of twice-exceptional children and adolescents. For example, the learning, social-emotional, and behavior difficulties present in twice-exceptional individuals depress their performance on intelligence tests. Consequently, the typical Full Scale IQ cutoff score of 130 used for the identification of giftedness is not sensitive enough to identify twice-exceptional students; and it is recommended that cutoff scores are adjusted downward (Nielsen, 2002). Research investigating the identification of gifted students with learning disabilities suggests the use of scatter and profile analysis in the identification of twice-exceptional individuals (Brody & Mills, 1997; Nielsen, 2002; Silverman, 2003). More specifically, Nielsen suggested that subtest scatter of at least seven scaled-score points between highest and lowest subtest scores on the Wechsler Intelligence test and low

Coding and Digit Span scores are indicative of twice-exceptionality; and they should be investigated further. Similarly, research investigating the identification of gifted students with social-emotional or behavior difficulties suggests that the use of Full Scale IQ scores is inappropriate in the identification of twice-exceptional children (Osborne & Byrnes, 1990).

To facilitate the identification of the twice-exceptional population, it is crucial that the ability profile of this group is investigated. The purpose of this research study is to contribute to this understanding by investigating the cognitive profile of twice-exceptional children and adolescents. An examination of the cognitive profile of twice-exceptional children and adolescents will not only contribute to improved identification and reduced misdiagnosis of this population, but will also contribute to more effective programming geared toward the specific needs of this population. Understanding the specific strengths and weaknesses of this population will aid in the planning of more comprehensive programs addressing both exceptionalities by fostering the strengths and talents of this group, while also providing accommodations for learning, behavioral, and social-emotional difficulties.

Cognitive Abilities

Research has examined the WISC factor and subtest score scatter of gifted children and gifted children with learning disabilities. No analysis has examined the cognitive ability of gifted students with behavioral or social-emotional difficulties. Research examining the discrepancy between verbal and performance IQ scores of gifted students has found large discrepancies with higher scores on the Verbal Scale (Patchett & Stansfield, 1992; Prifitera & Saklofske, 1998; Silver & Clampit, 1990). In contrast, studies investigating verbal-performance discrepancies among gifted students with learning disabilities have not found a discrepancy specific to this group but, instead, discovered mixed results (Barton & Starnes, 1989; Fox, 1983; Schiff, Kaufman, & Kaufman, 1981). As a result, no firm conclusion can be drawn regarding the verbal-performance discrepancy among twice-exceptional individuals; and additional research investigating this area is needed. In addition, verbal and performance scores are frequently viewed as obscuring an individual's cognitive ability because they combine several areas of functioning that may, therefore, lead to the averaging of strengths and weaknesses.

The publication of the Wechsler subtests provides clinicians and researchers the opportunity to analyze subtest score profiles instead of having merely to rely on a sole composite score. According to Kaufman (1994) and Sattler (2002), the WISC subtests have sufficient specificity (i.e., reliability and distinctiveness) to justify subtest analysis. Subtest analysis might be particularly meaningful to reach a better understanding of the areas of strength and weakness of the twice-exceptional population. In addition, subtest analysis is a recommended approach for the identification of this group, who may not demonstrate evenly developed cognitive abilities but may show gifts in some areas of functioning while demonstrating difficulties in others.

Research exploring the WISC subtest scatter of gifted children and adolescents has typically noted a great amount of scatter among subtests (Patchett & Stansfield, 1992; Schiff et al., 1981; Wilkinson, 1993). For example, Brown and Yakimowski (1987) found that gifted students commonly score lowest on the WISC-R subtests Coding and Digit Span, while the subtests Similarities, Comprehension, Information, and Block

Design are areas of strengths for these individuals. Investigating the subtest scatter of gifted students on the WISC-III, Fishkin, Kampsnider, and Pack (1996) found that these students showed a weakness on the Coding and Symbol Search subtests, while the subtests Similarities, Comprehension, and Vocabulary constituted areas of strength.

Limited research has investigated the cognitive ability of gifted students with learning disabilities. Research examining the subtest scatter among gifted students with learning disabilities indicates that this group scores lowest on the subtests Arithmetic, Coding, Information, and Digit Span and highest on the subtests Information, Similarities, Vocabulary and Comprehension (Baum, Owen, & Dixon, 1991; Schiff et al., 1981; Starnes, Ginevan, Stokes, & Barton, 1988). Barton and Starnes (1988) found different cognitive patterns among gifted students with mild and moderate vs. severe learning disability. The authors found that gifted students with mild and moderate learning disability scored higher on the Verbal vs. Performance Scale, while gifted students with severe learning disability showed higher Performance than Verbal IQ scores. An additional finding was that twice-exceptional students showed a greater amount of subtest scatter than the gifted group without learning disabilities. The results of the authors provide support regarding the heterogeneity of the twice-exceptional population. While this research suggests a cognitive pattern for gifted students with learning disabilities, no research has investigated the cognitive pattern of gifted students with behavioral or social-emotional difficulties. However, clinical studies investigating the cognitive profile of individuals with ADHD, ADD, or bipolar disorder revealed that these children demonstrate lower scores on the WISC-III Processing Speed and Freedom from Distractibility Indexes than the Verbal Comprehension and Perceptual Organization Index (Calhoun & Mayes, 2005; Mealer, Morgan, & Luscomb, 1996).

Cluster analysis is a promising technique that could be used to identify a typology of twice-exceptionality based on cognitive abilities. Several studies have cluster analyzed the WISC scores of learning disabled individuals and consistently found between five and six distinguishable learning disability subtypes. No cluster analyses have been performed investigating the WISC subtypes of gifted or twice-exceptional children. However, based on the heterogeneity of the twice-exceptional population, cluster analysis might be a promising tool for understanding this understudied population. The identification of twice-exceptional subtypes may not only increase understanding of this group, but may also lead to more effective identification, classification, and treatment of this population.

Problem Statement

Research exploring the cognitive processes of gifted students with learning disabilities has been limited, and studies investigating the ability profile of gifted students with behavior or social-emotional deficits are nonexistent. However, an investigation of the ability profiles of twice-exceptional children and adolescents is needed to understand the strengths and weaknesses of this group and to facilitate identification, reduce misdiagnosis, and improve service provision for this underserved population.

The purpose of this study is to explore the cognitive profiles of gifted children with learning, behavioral, and social-emotional difficulties. More specifically, this study investigates the ability scatter among twice-exceptional individuals to provide information about strengths and weaknesses of this group. In addition, based on the heterogeneity of this group, cluster analysis was used to discover specific subtype patterns present among twice-exceptional children and adolescents. Knowledge about the cognitive functioning of twice-exceptional children and adolescents will increase the understanding of this group, facilitate identification, reduce misdiagnosis, and aid in treatment and program planning of the twice-exceptional population.

CHAPTER 2

REVIEW OF THE LITERATURE

Children and adolescents who are intellectually gifted or have academic, social-emotional, and behavioral difficulties are typically viewed as belonging to large, distinct, and heterogeneous groups. Twice-exceptional children and adolescents belong to the domain where intellectual giftedness and academic, social-emotional, and/or behavioral difficulties interact, an area which is no less diverse, but in many cases, considerably more complex (Volker, Lopata, & Cook-Cottone, 2006). This literature review will begin with a discussion of the exceptionalities present in twice-exceptional children and adolescents: giftedness and problems in learning, behavior, or the social-emotional area. As an initial starting point, this literature review will more closely examine the construct of intellectual giftedness, including theories on the development of gifted children and adolescents, which will build a framework for a better understanding of the twice-exceptional population.

Giftedness

The definition of giftedness has proven to be a difficult task due to the field's confusion about what giftedness is, as well as little consensus in defining this construct from a conceptual viewpoint (Ackerman & Paulus, 1997; Brody & Mills, 1997). Lewis Terman is frequently considered the father of the gifted movement in the United States. In the 1920s, he initiated long-term studies of gifted students, who were colloquially referred to as *Termites*. He found that gifted children were taller, in better health, better developed physically, and better adapted socially than their peers. Terman's definition of giftedness included intelligence as a single criterion, and his studies focused on high-functioning individuals scoring in the top 1% on the Stanford-Binet Intelligence Scale (Tannenbaum, 1991). Leta Hollingworth (1928, 1943), a psychologist who studied giftedness around the same time as Terman, further contributed to understanding the intellectually gifted. Hollingworth found that children with IQ scores above 155 commonly suffer from adjustment problems, including social isolation and loneliness. Based on this discovery, which is quite contrary to Terman's description of gifted children as being well-adjusted in all areas of functioning, Hollingworth suggested that gifted individuals may be particularly vulnerable to certain psychosocial problems. This view laid the theoretical groundwork for an understanding of twice-exceptional children and adolescents.

Eventually, the concept of giftedness was expanded to include more complex, multi-faceted definitions. These definitions varied from a focus on intellectual ability (Sternberg, 1985), diverse abilities (Gardner, 1983), or the interactions among high ability, task commitment, and creativity (Renzulli, 1986). Marland (1972) proposed a multifaceted definition of giftedness describing individuals who possess high achievement or potential in any one of six areas, including general intellectual ability, specific academic domains, creative or productive thinking, leadership ability, visual and performing arts, and psychomotor ability. This view of giftedness has been adopted by the National Association for Gifted Children, the U.S. Department of Education, and most state departments of education and school systems (Brody & Mills, 1997). As is apparent in this definition of giftedness, a variety of abilities are recognized, extending far beyond a notion of simple academic ability. While Marland's definition of giftedness includes talents in several domains, this dissertation exclusively focuses on intellectual giftedness.

Theories of Development

Two theories conceptualizing the development of gifted students include Dabrowski's (1964) Theory of Positive Disintegration and Silverman's (1997) Theory of Asynchronous Development. These theories build a framework for understanding the characteristics of twice-exceptional children and adolescents.

Dabrowski's Theory of Positive Disintegration

The emotional development of gifted individuals has been described by Dabrowski's Theory of Positive Disintegration (1964, 1967). Kasimierz Dabrowski, a Polish psychiatrist, proposed that gifted individuals experience psychomotor, sensual, intellectual, imaginational, and emotional realms with heightened intensity and complexity. He termed an abundance of energy in any of these five areas as overexcitability. More specifically, he described overexcitabilites as a higher than average sensitivity of receptors in the psychomotor, sensual, imaginational, intellectual, or emotional domains. Consequently, individuals with overexcitabilites tend to view reality in a different and stronger manner that affects them more deeply and are long-lasting. Dabrowsky hypothesized that increased intensity, frequency, and duration of these overexcitabilities were indicative of a greater developmental potential, and therefore, show giftedness (Miller & Silverman, 1987). Dabrowsky's overexcitabilities can aid in the explanation of a number of difficulties faced by gifted children and adolescents.

Intellectual overexcitability. The area of intellectual overexcitability is characterized by a tendency to possess heightened curiosity, concentration, problem-solving capacity, and theoretical thinking ability. More specifically, individuals with this overexcitability have extremely active minds that desire to gain knowledge, understanding, and truth. They have a high degree of introspection and focus and enjoy contemplating moral concerns for extended periods of time. These independent thinkers and keen observers may become impatient if others do not share their enthusiasm about an idea.

Imaginational overexcitability. Imaginational overexcitability manifests itself in rich imagination, rich association, fantasy play, animistic thinking, daydreaming, dramatic perception, and use of metaphors. The majority of gifted children may tend to mix fantasy and reality and have one or more imaginary playmates or pets during their preschool years. As adults, these individuals display dramatic social interactions, daydreaming, and creativity.

Emotional overexcitability. Individuals who are emotionally overexcitable demonstrate an increased concern for and response to their environment. They show intense emotions such as compassion, empathy, and sensitivity, which can lead to temper tantrums and rage when they lose a game, feel left out, or do not get their way. In addition, they may have deep relationships, strong affective memory, self-evaluation, and a need for security. Their strong emotions, ranging from sadness to elation, are often viewed as extreme and puzzling by others in their lives.

Psychomotor overexcitability. Individuals with psychomotor overexcitability have an increased excitability of their neuromuscular system and are extremely active and energetic. These individuals enjoy movement and display rapid speech, intense physical activity, pressure for action, impulsiveness, and restlessness.

Sensual overexcitability. Individuals with sensual overexcitability possess a heightened sense of seeing, smelling, tasting, touching, and/or hearing. These individuals may feel overwhelmed by how their clothing feels on their body, by the view of fluorescent light, by the smell of perfume, or by the texture or taste of certain foods.

Silverman's Theory of Asynchronous Development

The term *asynchronous development* is used to describe giftedness as being out-of-sync with oneself, both internally and externally. This view is based on a child-centered perspective drawn from the works of Hollingworth, Vygotsky, Dabrowski, and Terrassier (Silverman, 1997). According to the Columbus Group, gifted individuals experience advanced cognitive abilities and heightened intensity, which create inner experiences quite distinct from those encountered by the normal population (Silverman, 1998). Gifted individuals experience discrepancies among various facets of their development. For example, a 7-year-old gifted child may show the reading ability of a child at the eighth grade level, the math ability of a child at the sixth grade level, and the fine-motor skills of someone at the second grade level. Also, gifted children may possess the intellectual capacity of adults, while their emotional maturity is still that of a child. They may understand abstract concepts such as right and wrong or evil to an advanced degree, yet may not possess the emotional maturity to manage that awareness. Hence, gifted children and adolescents may experience "a lack of synchronicity in the rates of their cognitive, emotional, and physical development" (Morelock, 1992, p. 11), which can create great inner tension. Typically, the greater the discrepancy between an individual's cognitive and physical development, the more likely he or she feels out-of-sync internally and in social relationships (Silverman, 1997).

The asynchrony frequently present in gifted students can be reflected in a great amount of scatter on IQ subtest scores, which may range from low average to very superior (Webb et al., 2005). Research indicates that this asynchronous development may lead to a variety of adjustment difficulties and frustration due to the great differences in ability these individuals experience. For example, a child may be able to visualize a finished product, but due to undeveloped motor skills, may not be able to implement the task. Frequently, these individuals have a particular awareness of tasks that are more challenging for them; and they tend to connect their areas of difficulties to their feelings of self-worth. This tendency, connected with their perfectionism and their all-or-none thinking, can foster a belief of *I cannot do anything right*, leading to feelings of despair, alienation, or depression (Webb et al., 2005).

Dabrowski's and Silverman's theories of development as they pertain to the gifted child and adolescent provide a lens into the development of this population that is quite distinct from the stereotypical portrayal of the gifted individual as being well adjusted in all areas of development. In contrast, these theories provide frameworks to conceptualize the difficulties this group may experience and are particularly applicable to the twice-exceptional population, which experiences areas of strength and weaknesses to a particular degree.

Twice-Exceptionality

Gifted children and adolescents who also exhibit learning, behavioral, or social-emotional problems exhibit characteristics of two exceptionalities: talents or strengths in some areas and difficulties in others. Gifted behaviors may include high levels of creativity, superior abstract thinking abilities, problem-solving prowess, and keen interests. Yet, these children may also experience social-emotional and behavioral difficulties such as feelings of depression, inadequacy, low self-esteem, diminished self-efficacy, loneliness, anger, and acting-out behaviors, as well as learning difficulties (NAGC, 1998).

The earliest accounts of the twice-exceptional population in the literature were provided through biographical sketches of eminent individuals, rather than through empirical study. For example, Thompson (1971) noted indications of gifted individuals suffering from learning difficulties. He suggested that Albert Einstein did not speak until he was 3 years old and suffered from spelling and writing difficulties into adulthood. Moreover, Thompson proposed that Woodrow Wilson did not learn to read until he was 11 years old and that Harvey Cushing, August Rodin, George Patton, and Thomas Edison all had some degree of reading, writing, and spelling retardation in their early lives.

Despite biographical evidence of twice-exceptional individuals and first descriptions of these children by educators, gifts and deficits were still viewed as being at opposite ends of a spectrum; and joining these two concepts was therefore regarded as resulting in an apparent contradiction (Baum & Owen, 2004). This view was mainly due to Terman's (1925) definition of giftedness, which conceptualized gifted children as being good at everything and as scoring uniformly high on intelligence tests. Such *stereotypic expectations interfered with the identification of potential gifts in students,* who were not high achievers in the classroom due to social-emotional or behavioral problems. Over the years, Terman's narrowly focused view of giftedness was expanded and resulted in a definition of giftedness that no longer excluded children with learning, social-emotional, or behavioral problems. Revised definitions of giftedness highlighted that children do not need to be exceptional in every area to be considered gifted, and that children can be gifted if they have potential but are not performing at a high level (Baum & Owen, 2004).

Research in the area of twice-exceptionality began following the Education of All Handicapped Children Act in 1975, which described a broadening emphasis on the education of students with disabilities (U. S. Office of Education, 1977). A colloquium held at John Hopkins University in 1981 including experts from both fields considering this issue concluded that students who are gifted yet also possess difficulties in some areas exist but are often overlooked. Following the colloquium, an article based on the proceedings of the conference was published in 1983; yet, no clear working definition of the twice-exceptional population was offered. Moreover, while the concomitant occurrence of giftedness and learning, behavior, or social-emotional difficulties has become more commonly accepted in recent years, empirical research investigating this area is still limited. In addition, the limited research that exists in the area of twice-exceptionality largely relies on case studies, observations, and self-reports rather than on findings from systematic empirical investigations (Cohen & Vaughn, 1994; Vaughn, 1989). Furthermore, the bulk of research in the area of twice-exceptionality has been conducted on the co-occurrence of giftedness and learning disability, while the areas of behavior and social-emotional difficulties have been studied less thoroughly.

Three groups of twice exceptional students can be recognized based on the co-occurrence of giftedness and areas of difficulty (NAGC, 1998). The first group includes students who have been identified as gifted but whose talents compensate for their difficulties; therefore, they are likely overlooked. These individuals may struggle as academic demands increase; but with their unrecognized learning, behavior, or social-emotional difficulties, their academic problems are likely attributed to a lack of motivation or a poor self-concept. The second group consists of students whose area of difficulty is recognized, but whose gift has not been identified. These students typically receive services to cope with their difficulties, but their areas of strength remain unsupported. The third and perhaps largest group includes unidentified students, whose gifts and difficulties mask or hide each other. These students typically perform at an average level and are therefore not recognized as having special needs; yet, they are performing well below their potential.

Empirical data reporting the actual incidence of twice-exceptional children and adolescents are virtually nonexistent. Prevalence estimates indicate that 2% to 5% of the total population of children with disabilities is also gifted. However, authors caution that these estimates are very conservative and that many students may remain hidden, being viewed as underachievers or average learners (Nielsen, 2002).

Areas of Deficits: Learning Problems, Behavior Problems, and Social-Emotional Difficulties

Learning Problems

The earliest accounts of learning disability in the literature appeared in the late 1940s, in which learning disability was associated with minimal brain injuries before, during, or after birth and affecting the neuromotor system. A decade later, the conception of learning disability was modified and traced to neurological dysfunctions or central processing disorders rather than brain injuries. Within a few years, this conceptualization was again adjusted to provide a definition that would have meaning for practice and intervention. In the early 1960s, the term was viewed as descriptive of children with disorders in receptive language, speech, reading, and communication skills. Learning disabilities were regarded as resulting from underlying language learning problems stemming from perceptual or cognitive processing difficulties. The definition's new focus on learning rather than neurology led to an expansion of its boundaries for the inclusion of a broader range of students (Baum & Owen, 2004).

In 1975, after much debate and compromise, the federal government passed PL 94-142 (The Education for All Handicapped Children Act), which defined learning disabled children as those suffering from a disorder that may manifest itself in listening, thinking, speaking, reading, writing, spelling, or mathematical difficulties (U.S. Office of Education, 1977). In 1990, PL 94-142 was amended and termed the Individuals with Disabilities Education Act (IDEA), whose purpose was to ensure appropriate diagnosis and educational accommodations for individuals with learning disabilities. According to its latest version (IDEA 2004), learning disabilities are defined as a disorder in one or more basic psychological processes with associated inclusive and exclusionary criteria. Most commonly, measures of an individual's ability or potential are compared to his or her achievement. If the individual's achievement falls significantly below his or her estimated ability, then a learning disability is suspected (Webb et al., 2005).

Three primary Learning Disorders, including Reading Disorder, Mathematics Disorder, and Disorder of Written Expression, as well as several Communication Disorders such as Expressive Language Disorder or Mixed Receptive-Expressive Language Disorder are noted in the *Diagnostic and Statistical Manual of Mental Disorders* (4th ed., text rev.; American Psychiatric Association, 2000). While any of these learning disorders can co-occur with giftedness, Communication Disorders are very uncommon in gifted individuals (unless there has been brain trauma) and are therefore not considered for the purpose of this dissertation.

Reading disorder. A common term for Reading Disorder is dyslexia. The essential feature of the disorder is reading achievement substantially below what would be expected given the individual's age, measured intelligence, and education. Children suffering from this disorder reverse, distort, substitute, or omit letters and show delays in learning to read (APA, 2000). Three types of dyslexia are noted. In the first type, individuals are able to read words correctly, yet are unaware of their meaning. Thus, these individuals are unable to make a connection between written words and their significance. This difficulty can be caused by a failure to understand the construction of language. In the second type, *surface dyslexia*, individuals are able to read regular but not irregular words, such as *yacht* or *buoy*, which break many of the conventions of phonological rules. In the third type, *deep dyslexia*, children are able to retrieve the right general concept from read words, but pronounce the wrong word, such as saying *car* when the printed word *automobile* is read (Webb et al., 2005).

Mathematics disorder. The essential feature of this disorder is mathematical ability substantially below what would be expected given the individual's chronological age, intelligence, and education. This disorder may be difficult to recognize before second grade because skills in mathematics are frequently not emphasized before then. In children with high overall intellectual ability, talents may compensate these difficulties; and the disorder may not be apparent until fifth grade or later. Specific functions that are typically affected by this disorder include linguistic skills (understanding or naming mathematical terms) attention skills (copying numbers correctly), perceptual skills (recognizing numerical symbols or arithmetic signs), and mathematical skills (mastering multiplication tables) (APA, 2000).

Disorder of written expression. The essential feature of this disorder includes writing skills substantially below what would be expected given the individual's age, measured intelligence, and education. Individuals with this disorder may display a combination of difficulties in their ability to compose written texts. Challenges may include grammatical or punctuation errors, poor paragraph organization, spelling errors, and poor handwriting (APA, 2000).

A further area of learning difficulties commonly observed in the twice-exceptional population involves nonverbal learning disabilities. Nonverbal learning disability means that the primary areas of deficit are in the nonverbal domains, which include difficulties in the area of attention, executive functioning, and auditory processing (Baum & Owen, 2004). Nonverbal learning disorders frequently go undiagnosed for a large part of a child's schooling, and children with this disability are commonly labeled as *emotionally disturbed* due to their inappropriate and unexpected conduct. As preschoolers, these children may show difficulty interacting with their peers, decreased exploratory skills, and difficulty acquiring self-help skills. In their elementary-school years, these children typically struggle with fine motor skills, attention, following directions, and anxiety. They may be accused of being lazy, rude, uncooperative, or unmotivated. The language development of these children may appear advanced due to extensive vocabulary and fluent speaking; however, these individuals typically struggle with the pragmatic features of language and may be unable to conduct interactive conversations (Voeller, 1994).

Attention difficulties. Attention-Deficit Disorder (ADD) with or without hyperactivity (ADHD) includes symptoms of inattention, impulsivity, and hyperactivity (APA, 2000). ADHD is the most common behavior disorder of childhood and is considered a severe public health problem by the National Institute of Health. Attention difficulties can include deficits in simple focus, sustaining attention over time, sustaining attention under distraction, shifting attention between tasks, or allocating attention wisely. Impulsivity problems include high levels of fidgeting, squirming, often being on the go, talking excessively, difficulty awaiting turns, and interrupting or intruding on others. Attention and impulsivity problems typically occur in several situations such as the home, community, and school setting.

It is important to acknowledge that giftedness and ADD/ADHD can co-occur because some professionals falsely hold the opinion that these conditions cannot co-exist. The correct diagnosis of both conditions is additionally hindered by the fact that the presence of both exceptionalities can obscure each other and obstruct the recognition of each. For example, the high intellectual ability of these children and adolescents may enable them to perform well on tests and assignments despite the fact that they are only able to attend to portions of the class period. For other children, attention and impulsivity may depress their scores on intelligence tests and their academic performance in the classroom. Moreover, teachers may tend to focus on the disruptive behaviors of twice-exceptional children and may therefore fail to recognize indicators of high cognitive ability. In addition, gifted children with ADD/ADHD present diagnostic and treatment dilemmas based on their ability to perform when there is structure and intrinsic motivation and an inability to even master the most simple and mundane task at other times (Webb et al., 2005). Children who are gifted and also suffer from ADD/ADHD need educational accommodations for their giftedness and treatment for their attention difficulties. Delays in the identification of these students hinder early provision of appropriate services that are crucial for the academic and social success of this population.

The differentiation between true attention deficits from the range of temperament and behavior common among the gifted population is challenging. The intensity, drive, perfectionism, curiosity, and impatience commonly observed among gifted students may be mistaken as indicators of ADHD. Gifted students may experience symptoms of inattention when not appropriately challenged or increased energy levels in areas of interest that may be misdiagnosed as ADD/ADHD. However, although similarities exist between gifted students and twice-exceptional students, some of the defining features of ADD/ADHD are not typically associated with giftedness. For instance, gifted children with ADD/ADHD have difficulty sustaining attention in most tasks or play activities, while gifted students without the co-morbidity tire easily on boring, unchallenging tasks, but are able to sustain attention when working on tasks of their own choosing. Ideally, a diagnosis of gifted students with ADHD is made by a clinician familiar with childhood psychopathologies who also understands the normal range of developmental characteristics of gifted children (Webb et al., 2005).

Difficulties with executive functioning. Executive functioning, including planning, judgment, impulse control, delaying gratification, self-monitoring, attention, social adroitness, and tact is an area of difficulty for many gifted children and adolescents. The frontal lobes, the brain area associated with executive functioning, are the last to mature; and their development is not completed until an individual is 16 to 20 years old. In contrast, the brain areas involved in academic measures such as language, mathematics, and fine motor skills develop much earlier. Thus, the development of executive functioning frequently lags behind intellectual development. Typically, the brighter the individual, the greater is the gap between judgment and intellect. An additional factor contributing to difficulties in the area of executive functioning is that the intellectual curiosity of gifted individuals frequently overrides their judgment. Executive dysfunction belongs to one of the most overlooked contributors to academic, behavioral, and social problems (Ozonoff, 1998).

Auditory processing deficits. Students with auditory processing deficits have difficulty decoding the information that they receive orally. For example, these students may struggle to understand speech in noisy environments, follow directions, and discriminate similar-sounding speech sounds. As a result, these individuals need more time processing verbal communication. These children and adolescents spend much of their time and effort trying to screen out noises that most others can simply ignore without effort. This leads to fatigue, disinterest, avoidance, or acting out behaviors. In the classroom, these children may have difficulty with reading, spelling, and understanding orally presented information (Webb & Dietrich, 2005).

Behavior Problems

The curiosity, intensity, asynchronous development, sensitivity, and the lag of judgment behind intellect of gifted students can result in behavior problems such as intense power struggles, arguments, temper tantrums, or sibling rivalry. Gifted children and adolescents with behavior problems are often focused in their area of interest; and their arguments evolve around moral, ethical, or social issues. Their thinking style is black and white; and their behavior is stubborn, dismissive, and rebellious. They frequently do not possess the insight or experience to cope with the situations they encounter. The root of the anger and the behavior problems of these children often stems from a feeling that *nobody understands me* (Webb et al., 2005). These students may carry various diagnoses addressing their behavior problems including Oppositional Defiant Disorder, Conduct Disorder, Intermittent Explosive Disorder, or Disruptive Behavior Disorder Not Otherwise Specified (NOS). School psychologists often label these children and adolescents with an Emotional/Behavioral Disability (EBD).

Gifted students with behavioral problems frequently feel unchallenged in the school setting, which further escalates their behavioral problems. Also, these students tend to unpredictably engage and disengage in learning opportunities, which results in inconsistent academic performance and knowledge foundations. Further, research indicates that gifted students with behavior problems commonly are not recommended for gifted programs, or they are terminated from such programs because of their negative and/or destructive behaviors (Reis & McCoach, 2002). The culture of EBD is heavily influenced by a concentration on deficits and negative characteristics; and these individuals are frequently described by the "Destructive D's", such as "dysfunctional, difficult, deviant, disordered, disturbed, disappointing, delinquent, dropout, disruptive, and disorganized" (Gallagher, 1997, p. 2). A focus on the negative characteristics of children with EBD often precludes the recognition and identification of potential gifted behaviors. In addition, it seems incongruous that gifted behaviors and challenging or negative behaviors can co-exist in the same student. The lack of understanding of gifted students with behavior difficulties has led to a failure to recognize, properly identify, and develop programming for gifted students with behavior difficulties.

There is a particular danger for gifted students with behavior problems in that their giftedness remains unrecognized, and only their behavior difficulties are addressed. These children are often diagnosed as suffering from a behavior disorder, while their giftedness remains unrecognized. Unfortunately, as a consequence, focus is only placed on the negative behavior of these students, while their strengths are not addressed. This further adds to the risk of these students not receiving appropriate educational services addressing their talents, in addition to them dropping out of school. Furthermore, there is a danger for these students to succumb to a negative self-fulfilling prophecy if the sole focus of treatment becomes their negative behavior while their intellectual ability is neglected (Rizza & Morrison, 2003).

Social-Emotional Difficulties

A further area of difficulty frequently experienced by twice-exceptional individuals includes social-emotional difficulties such as poor self-concept, depression, emotional lability, hypersensitivity, poor self-efficacy, anxiety, high levels of frustration, and social problems (Baum, Cooper, & Neu, 2001; Baum & Olenchak, 2002; Mooney & Cole, 2000). Twice-exceptional children and adolescents may suffer from several social-emotional difficulties due to their unique development and needs. It has frequently been assumed that the presence of gifts in this population would serve as a protective factor, buffering them from social-emotional problems. Yet, this assumption has not been supported by research. On the contrary, giftedness has been found to pose an additional risk factor for social and emotional difficulties; and research indicates that mood disorders such as depression or Bipolar Disorder are more common among gifted individuals (Neihart, 1999; Piirto, 2004).

Twice-exceptional children are more likely to recognize their difficulties in social and academic areas, generating much psychological conflict (Stormont, Stebbins, & Holliday, 2001). Research indicates that twice-exceptional individuals frequently experience frustration, leading to emotional upset and feelings of depression. Also, gifted individuals are frequently empathic and feel the weight of the world on their shoulders, which can lead to depression as they realize their inability to make a difference in the condition of the world (Silverman, 1998). Perfectionism is an additional factor contributing to frustration or depression when gifted children and adolescents feel that none of their efforts are adequate. Due to high levels of perfectionism, gifted students may hold very high standards for their performance, which can result in avoidance, anxiety, and failure (Webb & Dietrich, 2005).

Twice-exceptional children commonly experience a low self-concept due to their difficulty in coping with their varied abilities. Frustration, anger, and resentment may not only influence the inner experiences of these children and adolescents, but can also influence relationships with peers and family members. Research indicates that gifted individuals frequently suffer loneliness and experience inner conflicts between their desire to fit in with peers and their own inner ideals (Silverman, 1993). While they would like to share their interests with their peers, they often find that their same-age peers are not interested in this advanced-level information. This may lead to rejection by their peers, which can result in hostility or arrogance in the gifted student (Baum et al., 2001). Alternatively, gifted students may feel that they need to hide their ability to be accepted by their peers; and they may deny their academic needs to satisfy social needs. These students may adopt a happy-go-lucky façade with their peers, although they may be plagued by self-criticism, self-doubt, and intensive self-analysis.

The characteristics of giftedness should be considered in the diagnosis and treatment of the mood disorders of twice-exceptional individuals. Characteristics of giftedness do not only contribute to diagnoses, but also hold implications that need to be considered when working with twice-exceptional students (Webb et al., 2005). Because of their increased risk for emotional and social difficulties, twice-exceptional children and adolescents can benefit from professional assistance to reconcile their frustrations and perceived failures, as well as to establish and maintain social relationships (Brody & Mills, 1997).

An additional diagnosis that can co-occur with giftedness is Asperger's Disorder, which includes impairment in social interaction and the development of restricted, repetitive patterns of behavior, interests, and activities (APA, 2000). Gifted students with Asperger's Disorder may show a particular strength on verbal tasks and memory, while struggling with interpersonal relationships and empathy. Gifted children and adolescents with Asperger's Disorder may primarily learn through memorization of facts but may struggle to apply this information in a meaningful and creative manner. The poor social awareness of these children and adolescents handicaps their development of peer relationships, and they are frequently viewed as odd and are commonly teased and ridiculed by their classmates. In addition, despite their high verbal skills, these students may have difficulty with their motor skills and are often described as being clumsy. Moreover, these individuals tend to prefer structure and routine and may be preoccupied with intense interests, sometimes to the point of obsessions and compulsions. In gifted children with Asperger's Disorder, asynchronous development can be particularly extreme, leading to behaviors that appear especially puzzling and strange (Webb et al., 2005).

Misdiagnosis

While disabilities can exist simultaneously with giftedness, the existence of overlapping characteristics and the cross-pollination of giftedness with a disability can result in the misidentification or over-identification of multiple syndromes. It is important to recognize that not all students labeled with learning, behavior, or social-emotional difficulties while also exhibiting cognitive strengths are necessarily displaying gifted behavior and meet criteria for twice-exceptionality. Likewise, learning, social-emotional, or behavior problems exhibited by gifted students should not automatically be viewed as disabilities. It is important that the degree to which the different characteristics are exhibited is carefully evaluated to avoid misdiagnosis.

For instance, a gifted individual with intellectual and psychomotor overexcitability may present similarly to someone suffering from ADD/ADHD. Individuals with overexcitabilities in these domains may, due to an eager curiosity, blurt out answers in class, jiggle their feet, fidget, and appear to be off task, which could lead to a misdiagnosis of ADD/ADHD. In addition, gifted individuals may exhibit symptoms of inattention, similar to ADHD, when they are bored or not appropriately challenged. These gifted individuals may tire easily during boring, repetitive, unchallenging activities, while they sustain attention when working on tasks of their own choosing (Webb et al., 2005).

Gifted students with behavior problems are frequently misdiagnosed as suffering from Oppositional Defiant Disorder, Conduct Disorder, Intermittent Explosive Disorder, or Disruptive Behavior Disorder NOS, while their giftedness remains unrecognized. For example, it is not uncommon for a gifted individual's intensity to be displayed in strong-willed behavior, which could lead to a misdiagnosis of ODD. These individuals may demonstrate a strong focus in their area of interest, and they may impose their strong opinions onto others. The effort of others to redirect their focus or get them to see a different point of view may lead to angry power struggles, resembling symptoms of ODD (Webb et al., 2005).

Similar misdiagnosis can occur in the social-emotional area. For example, sadness related to gifted children's disappointed idealism or feelings of loneliness and alienation may be mistaken as Major Depressive Disorder. A further frequent misdiagnosis is OCD, which may be given based on a gifted child's love to organize things or people into complex frameworks and schema (Webb et al., 2005).

Misdiagnosis, misidentification, or over-identification of diagnoses among gifted children is a particular risk given the limited research in the area of twice-exceptionality. Additional research exploring the co-occurrence of giftedness and learning, behavior, and social-emotional difficulties may facilitate the diagnosis of this often unidentified and misdiagnosed group. An aim of this study is to contribute to the understanding of this group to facilitate the diagnosis of the twice-exceptional population.

Identification

In this section, this literature review more closely examines the methods used to identify the twice-exceptional population, with a particular focus on the use of intelligence tests. First, the identification of gifted children and adolescents is discussed; then, the identification of twice-exceptional children and adolescents is more closely explored. While research has studied the identification of gifted children with learning disabilities, only one study was located that explored the identification of gifted students with behavior problems. In contrast, no study on the identification of gifted students with social-emotional difficulties could be found.

Identification of Giftedness

Traditionally, the use of intelligence tests has been viewed as the gold standard for the identification of giftedness. As mentioned previously, Terman, the father of the gifted movement in this country, was perfectly satisfied with defining giftedness as the possession of a very high IQ and used the Stanford-Binet intelligence test to identify the participants for his Genetic Study of Genius (Terman, 1925). IQ scores identified individuals who could process information in both verbal and performance areas in a way that was highly superior compared to the norm. The ideal of excellence as exhibited by individuals with these high test scores was crucial to early researchers of gifted behavior.

Since Terman, giftedness has generally been identified through the Full Scale IQ (FSIQ) score obtained on intelligence tests, typically with a minimum cut-off score of 2 standard deviations (SDs) above the mean, which is an FSIQ of 130 (Volker et al., 2006). Individuals with an FSIQ Score of 130-155 are labeled gifted, while individuals scoring at 155 or above are referred to as profoundly gifted. Yet, most current intelligence measures, such as the *Wechsler Intelligence Scale for Children*, only measure four *SD* units above the mean (an FSIQ of 160), thus not allowing high enough ceilings for individuals scoring well above the norms (Webb et al., 2005).

While intelligence tests are most typically used to identify gifted individuals, this conceptualization of intelligence has recently been criticized as narrow because intelligence tests do not adequately assess talents in areas such as leadership, musical, or physical talents. In addition, it has been increasingly recognized that FSIQ scores, which represent a composite, may average underlying abilities, and therefore, obscure strengths and weaknesses. Consequently, while FSIQ scores are still an important consideration in assessing intellectual giftedness, additional criteria such as a variety of cognitive abilities, creativity, and achievement motivation, as well as multiple sources, including grades, teacher nominations, test data, classroom observation, and parent reports are now frequently considered in identifying gifted individuals (Volker et al., 2006).

Despite the criticism of intelligence tests for the identification of giftedness, several factors promote their continued use. First, IQ measures meet the gold standard for psychometric reliability and validity. The FSIQ has been found to be remarkably dependable, both across time and internally among its component subtests. Furthermore, the norming samples of these measures are among the largest and most representative of the U.S. population of any test encountered. Additionally, intelligence tests remain the single most effective predictor of today's academic success, with the FSIQ score explaining approximately one quarter of the variability in performance at school. Intelligence tests are better predictors of success outside of classroom settings than any other single source (Anastasi, 1982; Cronbach, 1984). No other measures exist today that meet or surpass these criteria and that could, therefore, be utilized to replace IQ tests (Lovett & Lewandowski, 2006).

Second, while intelligence tests have rightfully been criticized for excluding several abilities such as artistic talent and physical agility, they have been deliberately designed to measure abilities that are most crucial in the environments that employ these tests, such as schools and educational programming (Lovett & Lewandowski, 2006). In these environments, intelligence tests can help educators understand the dimensions of students who qualify for special services because of their educational differences from the norm. Consequently, while the use of IQ measures as the sole criteria for gifted eligibility is inappropriate, these tests are currently the most adequate tool for defining giftedness; and their use in the identification of giftedness can still yield valuable diagnostic information (Nielsen, 2002).

Identification of Twice-Exceptionality

The identification of twice-exceptional children and adolescents is more problematic than the identification of giftedness alone, due to the co-existence of giftedness and learning, social-emotional, or behavior problems. While the use of intelligence tests, academic performance, teacher nominations, behavioral observations, and parent reports is typically adequate to identify gifted students, the identification of the twice-exceptional population warrants additional considerations due to a number of barriers that typically limit the identification of this group.

One barrier that has led to the misidentification of twice-exceptional children and adolescents includes stereotypical attitudes that a person with a deficit in one area cannot also be gifted. Professionals are frequently unaware that the characteristics of one exceptionality may overlap with other exceptionalities (Reid, 1995). The stereotypical view of gifted students that has prevailed since Terman's time is that gifted children and adolescents perform uniformly high on intelligence tests and do well in school. Consequently, the widely held belief that children with learning, behavioral, or social-emotional problems cannot also be gifted remains prevalent. The idea that gifted students may have deficits appears to be an oxymoron for most. For example, it may seem contradictory that an intellectually gifted child with a Full Scale IQ of 140 may struggle with handwriting or spelling. As a result, twice-exceptional students frequently remain unidentified and do not receive services to address their gifts and disabilities.

An additional barrier in the identification of twice-exceptional students is the false belief that these students will demonstrate the same characteristics as individuals with either exceptionality separately. Yet, it is crucial to recognize that disabilities and gifts frequently mask each other. The learning, social-emotional, or behavior problems present in these students depress their performance on intelligence tests; and these children therefore commonly go unrecognized as being gifted. For example, children who are gifted and also suffer from ADHD may have difficulty attending to an intelligence test and therefore receive an IQ score that underestimates their actual ability. As a result, they may fail to meet the definition of giftedness, particularly if based on an IQ cutoff score of 130 or above. At the same time, twice-exceptional students are often able to compensate for their deficits; and as a result, their deficits often remain unrecognized. For instance, in gifted children with ADHD, their giftedness may still allow them to score in the average range on an intelligence test; and their attention deficit may therefore remain unrecognized. Consequently, because gifts and difficulties obscure each other, twice-exceptional individuals frequently remain unidentified (Nielsen, 2002).

Due to the challenges in the identification of twice-exceptional students, several modifications have been offered. First, when identifying the presence of giftedness among this population, practitioners are cautioned that learning, social-emotional, or behavior problems can depress global intelligence scores of gifted students; therefore, cutoff scores of measures need to be adjusted downward (Brody & Mills, 1997). Nielsen (2002) argued that applying the typical requirement of an FSIQ of 130 for the identification of giftedness to the twice-exceptional population would be inappropriate and self-defeating. When FSIQ is employed as a single criterion for the provision of services, many twice-exceptional individuals with uneven patterns are denied services due to this misapplication of IQ data. It is therefore recommended that students who score at or slightly below 120 on an IQ test be further evaluated for any indicators of giftedness (Silverman, 1998).

Identification of Gifted Students with Learning Disabilities

Four research articles published in the past 10 years have specifically considered the identification of gifted students with learning disabilities. Other documents published on gifted children with learning disabilities have either referred to one of these four primary sources or did not substantively address the identification of gifted children and adolescents with a learning disability (Lovett & Lewandowki, 2006).

The first document considering the issue of identifying twice-exceptional individuals is a comprehensive review by Brody and Mills (1997). The authors concluded that three factors are of special importance when identifying gifted students with learning disabilities: (a) evidence of outstanding talents, (b) an aptitude-achievement discrepancy, and (c) processing deficits. Consequently, Brody and Mills suggested assessment procedures that include an integration of IQ scores with more subjective indices such as structured interviews, behavioral observations, creativity tests, and teacher nominations. More specifically, the authors suggested the use of scatter analysis, profile analysis, broad definitions of intelligence and giftedness, and ability-achievement discrepancy models of learning disabilities.

Further guidelines for the identification of twice-exceptional children and adolescents were proposed by McCoach, Kehle, Bray, and Siegle (2001). These authors sought to provide criteria for the diagnostic category of twice-exceptional students for practicing school psychologists. They suggested the use of the discrepancy conceptualization typically used to evaluate learning disabilities and additionally the use of IQ tests to differentiate twice-exceptional students from non-gifted students with learning disabilities. Yet, McCoach et al. were reluctant to suggest a specific IQ cutoff score. Contrary to other researchers, they did not endorse the use of scatter and profile analysis but agreed on the use of discrepancy models of learning disability.

An additional source discussing the identification of twice-exceptional children and adolescents is a study by Nielsen (2002). Based on test data gathered from the assessment files of more than 300 gifted students with learning disabilities, Nielsen suggested several assessment recommendations. Proposed recommendations included the using comprehensive psychoeducational batteries, an examination of discrepancies between performance on different measures, and flexibility in identification criteria such as cutoff scores. Particularly, Nielsen stressed that practitioners consider low scores on Coding and Digit Span subtests, as well as subtest scatter of at least seven scaled-score points between the highest and lowest subtest score on the Wechsler Intelligence Test as indicative of twice-exceptionality. In summary, Nielsen recommended the use of scatter analysis, profile analysis, broad definitions of giftedness, and discrepancy definitions of learning disability.

Finally, in an overview of twice-exceptional students, Silverman (2003) discussed the modification of standard assessment protocols when identifying this population. The author suggested that it is imperative to inspect separate subtest scores of twice-exceptional children because giftedness and learning disabilities frequently mask each other, thus making the consideration of solely a composite score unreliable. In accordance with Brody and Mills (1997) and Nielsen (2002), Silverman recommended the use of scatter analysis, profile analysis, broad definitions of giftedness, and use of the discrepancy model.

Identification of Gifted Students with Behavior or Emotional Problems

Research suggests that current screening and assessment practices frequently fail to identify gifted students with social-emotional and/or behavior difficulties (Morrison, 2001). Gallagher (1997) asserted that one problem in the identification of these individuals is that the rating scales used to identify students for EBD placement consist of simple behavior rating lists that exclude the assessment of strengths within an individual. This contributes to the risk that the behavior disability of twice-exceptional students becomes the main focus while their gifts remain unrecognized.

Osborne and Byrnes (1990) investigated the identification of gifted students with behavior problems. They examined the likelihood of gifted students being placed in an alternative learning center for children with disruptive or disaffected behaviors. These students were removed from their public schools; and their behaviors were described as being dull, disruptive, and rebellious. Of the 93 students examined in the study, 8% were identified as exhibiting potentially gifted behaviors. However, had an FSIQ score been used as the sole indicator of giftedness, not one student would have met the criteria for giftedness. In contrast, students were identified through teacher nomination, classroom observations, interviews, and a review of the student's work in addition to performance on IQ tests.

Due to the reported difficulties in recognizing, understanding, and identifying gifted students with behavior disabilities, Rizza and Morrison (2003) investigated the ability of teachers to recognize and identify students who are EBD and gifted. Results revealed stereotypical thinking in the identification of students labeled gifted and students labeled EBD. Gifted students were viewed as being successful, high achieving, and able to develop their own goals. In contrast, EBD students were viewed as having mood-swings, poor self-concepts and self-control, as well as being explosive, disruptive, rebellious, and dangerous. Results indicate that teachers may use stereotypes when judging the behaviors of exceptional students, which could result in the misidentification of twice-exceptional students whose gifts may be hidden by emotional or behavioral difficulties and who are then overlooked because of stereotypes. As a result, twice-exceptional students whose gifts remain unrecognized may not receive an educational program commensurate with their true abilities; instead, they may solely receive services addressing their difficulties.

Several screening and assessment procedures are recommended for the identification of gifted students among the EBD population. Recommended procedures entail multi-criteria assessments including ability assessment, portfolio assessment, teacher recommendations, and observations. In addition, Functional Behavioral Assessment (Fox, Gunter, Davis, & Brall, 2000) or strength based assessment tools (Epstein, 1999) with a focus on quantitative and qualitative data are recommended for providing a more complete description of gifted behaviors in students labeled EBD (Morrison, 2001).

In conclusion, the identification of twice-exceptional children and adolescents is difficult; and services frequently are not provided until these students experience significant problems. To facilitate the resilience of this population, it is crucial that identification procedures are improved to identify twice-exceptional children and adolescents as early as possible. Additional research investigating the ability profile of twice-exceptional students may add to understanding this group. This may facilitate the recognition, identification, and service provision to this often misidentified and misdiagnosed group. The aim of this research study is to add to this understanding by investigating the cognitive profile of twice-exceptional children and adolescents.

Educational Needs

The educational needs of twice-exceptional children and adolescents are quite distinct from those of the general population. Understanding the specific learning and motivational patterns of this population can aid in planning comprehensive programs for these students. Effective programs are aimed at fostering strengths, talents, and interests as well as providing accommodations and compensation strategies to minimize the effect of learning, social-emotional, and behavioral problems. In general, interventions should be aimed at providing positive effects on the education, health, and well-being of this group (Baum & Owen, 2004).

Educational misplacement of twice-exceptional children can lead to significant stress for these children as well as their families. Unfortunately, because no clear definitions exist that appreciate the unique characteristics and needs of twice-exceptional children and adolescents, these students frequently remain unidentified; and supportive programming or interventions serving this population remain sparse. Adding to this lack of services is the fact that, at the present time, the identifications of students for gifted programs and for special education services are mutually exclusive activities (Baum, 1994). As a consequence, twice-exceptional students usually fail to meet the eligibility requirements for either service, which is unfortunate, because these services can foster protective factors in this population that may ameliorate risk (Gardynik & McDonald, 2004).

Unless definition and identification criteria are modified to accommodate twice-exceptional individuals, this subgroup will continue to be excluded from needed services, which can lead to debilitating social and emotional consequences for this population (Brody & Mills, 1997). Twice-exceptional children, if misdiagnosed, are at risk for suffering from an intellectual poverty, substance abuse, and psychological difficulties if their exceptionalities are not recognized and addressed. Ideally, twice-exceptional individuals are evaluated and identified early, so that problems that otherwise would be overlooked can be addressed to prevent social and behavioral problems in this population. Early identification and appropriate intervention are valuable in reducing frustration and preventing plummeting self-esteem that often results when the needs of this group are overlooked (Webb et al., 2005).

An ideal learning environment for this population would focus on both exceptionalities by addressing difficulties, while at the same time focusing on talents and interests. Addressing students' abilities, rather than solely teaching to students' weaknesses can contribute to enhanced self-concepts, motivation, and task completion in these children and adolescents. Encouraging twice-exceptional students to understand their strengths and weaknesses and providing them with the skills needed to adapt to and compensate for weaknesses supplies them with the cognitive thinking, formal logic, and problem-solving tools needed to help them appraise learning situations and themselves. Employing these skills provides twice-exceptional students with control, encourages positive social-emotional development, and furthers their ability to overcome adversity (Gardynik & McDonald, 2004).

Cognitive Abilities

This literature review will now focus on a comprehensive discussion of the cognitive abilities of twice-exceptional children and adolescents. First, a review of the Wechsler Intelligence Scale for Children is provided, with a particular focus on the third and fourth editions. Second, the cognitive abilities of gifted and twice-exceptional children are more closely examined. This will entail a review of the ability profile of this population including scatter, profile, and cluster analyses that have been conducted by previous research.

To better understand and serve twice-exceptional children and adolescents, it is important to gain an increased comprehension of the perceptual patterns and cognitive abilities of this population. A better understanding of students' cognitive strengths and weaknesses may allow professionals to access students' stronger processing modalities while providing remedial services in weaker areas (Waldron & Saphire, 1990). The examination of the cognitive abilities of twice-exceptional students is typically derived from an inspection of the ability patterns on intelligence tests such as the *Wechsler Intelligence Scale for Children* (WISC), one of the most widely used intelligence measures (Wechsler, 1974). Results of such examinations can provide a clue into the learning patterns of this group of students (Baum & Owen, 2004).

Wechsler Intelligence Scale for Children

The Wechsler Intelligence Scale for Children was designed as an assessment tool for global intelligence. Wechsler (1949) conceptualized intelligence as an individual's capacity to understand and adapt to the world around him or her and viewed his intelligence scales to capture this ability. According to Wechsler, intelligence is an aggregate of an individual's capacity to act purposefully, think rationally, and manage effectively his or her world (Wechsler, 1974). The Wechsler Intelligence Scales are an attempt to measure an individual's general intelligence and to distinguish between verbal and nonverbal abilities.

The first Wechsler ability test for children was published in 1949 as the Wechsler Intelligence Scale for Children (WISC) and represented mainly a downward extension of the Wechsler-Bellevue Intelligence Scale, Form II for adults. Since the inception of the WISC, there have been three revisions: the WISC-R, WISC-III, and WISC-IV. The first revision, the WISC-R occurred in 1974 and included several alterations. Obsolete or ambiguous test items were removed, new test items that would strengthen the WISC-R reliability were added, the test's standardization was updated with the most recent national census, and the age range of the test was changed from 5 through 15 years to 6 through 16 years (Wechsler, 1949).

The WISC-R and WISC-III contain three scales, the Full Scale IQ (FSIQ), the Verbal IQ (VIQ), and the Performance IQ (PIQ), each with a mean of 100 and a standard deviation of 15. The tests are constructed of subtests that comprise Verbal and Performance Scales and that can further be compiled into factor scores. The WISC-IV no longer contains the division in VIQ and PIQ, but simply uses FSIQ and four factor index scores.

The Verbal IQ measures intellectual functioning based on verbal comprehension, which includes the application of verbal skills and information to solve new problems, process verbal information, and think with words. The Verbal Scale further provides information about an individual's language processing, reasoning, attention, verbal learning, and memory. VIQ is affected by a child's motivation, previous education, interests, cultural opportunities, natural endowment, and acculturation. The Performance IQ measures perceptual organization, including an individual's ability to think in visual images, to manipulate these images, to reason without the use of words, and to interpret visual material quickly. The PIQ assesses an individual's visual processing, planning and organizational ability, attention, nonverbal learning, and memory. VIQ is further affected by motivation, interests, cultural opportunities, natural endowment, attention span, ability to process visual information, and psychomotor ability (Sattler, 2001).

Several researchers conducted factor analyses on the WISC to group the WISC subscales into meaningful categories. Rapaport, Gill, and Schafer (1946) presented a dichotomy of the nonverbal subtests, including the Visual Organization group (Picture Completion and Picture Arrangement), which requires visual-perceptual awareness, and the Motor Coordination subtests (Block Design, Object Assembly, Coding), which are dependent on integration of perceptual-motor skills.

Bannatyne (1974) recategorized the WISC-R subtests and identified four factors, including Verbal Conceptualization, Sequencing, Acquired Knowledge, and Spatial Ability. The Verbal Conceptualization factor includes the subtests Similarities, Vocabulary, and Comprehension from the Verbal Scale and covers the abilities related to language development. The Spatial Ability factor includes the subtests Picture Completion, Block Design, and Object Assembly, and samples the ability to manipulate objects in multidimensional space, either directly or symbolically. It tends to be the factor least dependent on special educational or cultural opportunities and can, therefore, be applied to various populations. The Acquired Knowledge factor includes Information, Arithmetic, and Vocabulary subtests, which are influenced by school and home environment and involve long-term memory. The Sequencing factor, also called Freedom from Distractibility factor or Third Factor, includes the subtests Arithmetic, Digit Span, and Coding. It measures the ability to retain and use sequences of auditory and memory stimuli in short-term memory.

Several problems with Bannatyne's four factors were identified (Schiff et al., 1981). First, the Acquired Knowledge subtests were found to overlap with other factors. More specifically, the Arithmetic subtest was shared with the Sequencing factor, while the Vocabulary subtest was shared with the Verbal Conceptualization factor. Kaufman (1975, 1979) endeavored to refine the factors for the WISC-R standardization sample; and an analysis rendered the following factors: Verbal Comprehension, Perceptual Organization, Right Brain Processing, Left Brain Processing, Integrated Functioning, and Organic Brain Syndrome. The Verbal Comprehension factor includes the subtests Information, Similarities, Vocabulary, and Comprehension and measures the ability necessary for item content (verbal) and mental process (comprehension). The Perceptual Organization factor includes the subtests Picture Completion, Picture Arrangement, Block Design, Object Assembly, and Mazes and measures the ability for item content (perceptual) and mental process (organization). The Right Brain Processing factor includes the subtests Picture Completion and Object Assembly and is hypothesized to measure right-hemisphere function, involving visuospatial tasks such as orientation and localization. The Left Brain Processing factor includes Information, Similarities,

Arithmetic, Vocabulary, and Comprehension and is hypothesized to measure left-hemisphere function, involving verbal ability. The Integrated Functioning factor includes Picture Arrangement, Block Design, Coding, and Mazes. In addition, Wechsler proposed a further factor, Organic Brain Syndrome (Digit Span, Coding, Block Design) because he noted, based on the standardization sample, that low scores on this factor may be indicative of brain dysfunction. Thus, he suggested that low scores on this factor be investigated further through more in-depth neurological testing. Kaufman (1979) noted that no one factor grouping was necessarily better than another but that it depended on what the investigator wanted to emphasize when testing different individuals or groups.

FSIQ, VIQ, PIQ and factor index scores of the WISC are derived from combining the 10 core subtest scores, which have a mean of 10 and a standard deviation of 3. The WISC subtests were designed to assess global intelligence in as many ways as possible. The subtests are reflective of Wechsler's belief that intelligence is a multidetermined, multifaceted entity. Wechsler noted that no one subtest was meant to depict all intellectual behavior (Wechsler, 1991). The seven categories used to characterize IQ scores consist of Very Superior (130 and above), Superior (120-129), High Average (110-119), Average (90-109), Low Average (80-89), Borderline (70-79), and Intellectually Deficient (69 and below) (Wechsler, 1991).

Wechsler Intelligence Scale for Children, Third Edition (WISC-III)

The WISC-III was the second revision of the WISC and occurred in 1991 (Wechsler, 1991). The goals of the revision were to enhance the factor structure of the WISC-III, to minimize test bias based on gender and ethnicity, to develop supplemental materials such as a co-normed achievement test, and to improve the subtests, such as by increasing floor and ceiling. In addition, a new test, the Symbol Search subtest, was added to the Performance Scale.

As mentioned previously, subtests comprise a Verbal and Performance Scale. The Verbal Scale is comprised of five mandatory and one supplementary subtest including Information, Similarities, Arithmetic, Vocabulary, Comprehension, and Digit Span (Sattler, 2001).

Information. The student is orally presented with a number of questions that assess a general fund of knowledge about common events, objects, places, people, and facts. The information subtest measures the knowledge a child has acquired through natural endowment, formal and informal education, and cultural opportunities, experiences, and interests. Provided with average opportunities, the average child should have acquired the knowledge sampled by this subtest through typical home and school experiences. High scores on the information subtest require memory for habitual, overlearned material to which the child was likely exposed repeatedly; thus, the subtest provides clues about a child's ability to store and retrieve acquired knowledge.

Similarities. The student is presented orally with a series of word pairs and asked to explain the relationship between the words. The similarities subtest measures verbal concept formation, the ability to meaningfully group objects and events. In addition to perceiving the common elements of the word pairs with which the child is presented, the child must merge the common elements into a concept. Thus, the child may need to organize, abstract, and find relationships that are not immediately evident. Additional factors contributing to a child's performance on this subtest include cultural opportunities, interest patterns, and memory.

Arithmetic. The student is orally presented with arithmetic problems and asked to solve them mentally. The Arithmetic subtest measures the child's ability to follow verbal directions, concentrate on selected parts of the problem, hold information in working memory, and use numerical operations. As a result, this subtest measures non-cognitive functions (concentration and attention) in combination with cognitive functions (knowledge of numerical operations). Additional factors contributing to a child's performance on this subtest include education interests, memory, prior learning, and the ability to actively apply selected skills to unique situations.

Vocabulary. The student is given a word and asked to provide the oral definition of the word. Words are arranged in order of increasing difficulty. The vocabulary subtest, a test of word knowledge measures a child's learning ability, fund of information, richness of ideas, memory, concept formation, and language development. The vocabulary subtest is considered to be an excellent estimate of a child's intellectual ability due to its assessment of a child's capacity to learn and accumulate information. Performance on this subtest has been found to be stable over time and relatively resistant to neurological deficit and psychological disturbance, thus providing useful information about a child's general cognitive ability.

Comprehension. The student is asked a series of questions that access his or her understanding of social rules, ethical judgment, and concepts. The comprehension subtest measures a child's possession of practical information and his or her ability to utilize previous experience. The subtest particularly focuses on a child's knowledge of conventional standards or behavior, extensiveness of cultural opportunities, and level of moral development. High performance on this subtest suggest common sense, social judgment, and a grasp of social conventionality, which are believed to measure a child's capacity to use facts in a pertinent, meaningful, and emotionally appropriate manner.

Digit span. This is a supplementary subtest in which the student is given a series of numbers and asked to repeat them forward or backwards. Digit Span particularly assesses a child's short-term sequential auditory memory and attention. More specifically, the subtest requires a child to retain several elements that do not have a logical relationship, to recall auditory information, and to verbally repeat the information in proper sequence. Digit Span Forward mainly assesses a child's sequential processing and short-term memory ability. In contrast, Digit Span Backwards requires more complex cognitive processing involving both planning ability and sequential processing. More specifically, Digit Span Backward requires the child to transform stimuli prior to responding, thus, requiring the child to hold the mental image while he or she mentally manipulates the sequence before restating it verbally. High scores on Digit Span Backward suggest flexibility, good stress tolerance, and excellent concentration.

In addition to the Verbal IQ, the Full Scale IQ includes the Performance IQ. The Performance IQ consists of five mandatory and two supplementary subtests that require students to solve problems using manipulation of visual stimuli (Sattler, 2001).

Picture completion. The student is shown pictures with an important part missing and asked to indicate the missing part verbally or through pointing. Picture Completion requires the child to recognize the depicted object, appreciate its incompleteness, and determine the missing part, hence, assessing a child's visual discrimination ability, the capacity to differentiate between essential and nonessential detail. Additional concepts assessed by this subtest include concentration, reasoning, visual organization, and long-term visual memory.

Coding. The student is asked to copy geometric symbols that are paired with other symbols or numbers. The Coding subtest requires the child to inspect each digit, locate the digit in the proper table, code the information distinguishing the symbol, and carry this information in short-term memory long enough to reproduce the symbol in the proper answer box. The speed and accuracy with which the child performs this task is hypothesized to measure the child's intellectual ability. Concepts assessed by the Coding subtest include a child's ability to learn an unfamiliar task, speed and accuracy of visual-motor coordination, speed of mental operation (processing speed), attention skills, visual acuity, visual scanning, visual tracking, short-term memory for new learning (learning of an unfamiliar code), cognitive flexibility (rapidly shifting from one pair to another), handwriting speed, and motivation. High performance on this subtest is not only influenced by comprehension of the task, but also by fine motor skills and visuoperceptual ability.

Picture arrangement. The student is given a series of pictures and asked to place them in a sequential order to tell a story that makes sense. The Picture Arrangement subtest assesses a child's ability to comprehend and evaluate a situation. High performance on the subtest is believed to measure a child's appraisal of the total situation depicted and his or her ability to grasp the general idea of a story. More specifically, Picture Arrangement is hypothesized to measure a child's nonverbal reasoning ability, including planning, anticipation, visual organization, and temporal sequencing. Thus, this subtest assesses a child's ability to anticipate, interpret, judge, and understand the possible antecedents and consequences of events and social situations.

Block design. The student is required to look at pictures of abstract designs and to reproduce them using three-dimensional blocks. The Block Design subtest involves analysis and synthesis ability by requiring a child to perceive and analyze forms by breaking down a whole design into its parts and then assembling its components into an identical design. Concepts required to perform this task involve visual organization, abstract conceptualization, visual-motor coordination, logic, and reasoning. Consequently, Block Design is considered to be a nonverbal concept-formation task involving perceptual organization and spatial visualization. A child's performance on this subtest may be influenced by motor activity and vision.

Object assembly. The student is asked to assemble jigsaw puzzle pieces to form a recognizable whole as quickly as possible. The Object Assembly subtest assesses a child's synthesis skills (putting parts together to form familiar objects), visual organization (anticipating relationships among individual parts), visual-motor coordination (recognizing individual parts and placing them correctly in the incomplete figure), motor activity, persistence, and long-term visual memory (stored information about the object to be formed).

Symbol search. This is a supplementary subtest in which the student is required to scan objects in a target and search group and to indicate whether or not a target symbol appears in the search group. More specifically, the subtest requires a child to inspect each item for the target stimulus, look at the array of items, determine whether the target stimulus is present among the array of items, and mark the appropriate YES or NO box once a decision is made. The Symbol Search subtest is a measure of perceptual discrimination, speed and accuracy, visual attention and concentration, short-term memory, and cognitive flexibility (shifting rapidly from one array to the next). Similar to the Coding subtest, speed and accuracy with which the task is performed are hypothesized to measure a child's intellectual ability.

Mazes. This is a supplementary subtest that requires students to complete a series of progressively more difficult paper/pencil mazes. The Mazes subtest requires a child to attend to, remember, and execute the direction including locating a route, avoiding blind alleys, crossing no lines, and holding the pencil on the paper. Mazes measures a child's planning ability, perceptual-organizational ability (the ability to plan and follow a visual pattern), visual-motor coordination, speed, and accuracy.

With the WISC-III, the overreliance on verbal and performance IQ scores was largely reduced, with the test providing four factor-analysis based index scores: Verbal Comprehension (Information, Similarities, Vocabulary, Comprehension), Perceptual Organization (Picture Completion, Picture Arrangement, Block Design, Object Assembly), Freedom from Distractibility (Arithmetic, Digit Span), and Processing Speed (Coding, Symbol Search). The optional subtest Mazes is not included in the calculation of any of the IQ or factor index scores.

The Verbal Comprehension Index (VCI) is hypothesized to measure a verbal-related ability underlying item content (verbal) and mental processes (comprehension). The VCI assesses verbal knowledge and understanding attained through formal and informal education, as well as the ability to apply verbal skills to new situations. The Perceptual Organization Index (POI) is hypothesized to measure a performance-related ability underlying item content (perceptual) and mental process (organization). POI assesses an individual's ability to interpret and organize visually perceived material within a time constraint. The Freedom from Distractibility Index (FDI) is hypothesized to measure a memory-related ability underlying item content (verbal) and mental processes (memory). FDI assesses an individual's ability to sustain attention, concentrate, and exert mental control. The Processing Speed Index (PSI) is hypothesized to measure a processing speed ability underlying item content (perceptual) and mental process (speed). PSI measures an individual's ability to process nonverbal information quickly, to concentrate, and to utilize rapid eye-hand coordination (Sattler, 2001). PSI is a new factor that is not found in previous versions of the WISC and has the lowest correlation with the FSIQ (.58) in comparison to the other factors (VCI .90, POI .88, and FDI .68) in the WISC-III standardization sample. This indicates that PSI is more independent of IQ than the other factors (Wechsler, 1991). Kaufman (1992) cited the timed nature of the performance sections of the WISC-III as a possible negative factor that could suppress a child's intelligence score. He particularly viewed PSI as a penalizing factor for gifted children who tend to be reflective and perfectionistic and may work at a slower pace. As a result, processing speed is not as large a factor in the WISC-IV; however, it may still present an area of weakness for gifted children and adolescents and therefore depress the IQ scores of this population.

Wechsler Intelligence Scale for Children, Fourth Edition (WISC-IV)

The WISC-IV was published in 2003 and is the most current version of the Wechsler Intelligence Scale. Revisions from the WISC-III to the WISC-IV are more numerous than previous revisions to the instrument. The most notable change includes the previously mentioned omission of the traditional Verbal vs. Performance Scales in favor of the four composite scores: Verbal Comprehension Index (VCI), Perceptual Reasoning Index (PRI), Working Memory Index (WMI), and Processing Speed Index (PSI) to better represent cognitive functioning. However, according to Wechsler (2003), the Verbal Comprehension and Perceptual Reasoning indices on the WISC-IV can be substituted for the Verbal and Performance IQ in the WISC-III. The age range of the WISC-IV remained at the WISC-III range of 6:00 through 16:11 years (Wechsler, 2003).

The five primary revision goals of the WISC-IV included: (a) updating the instrument's theoretical foundations, (b) enhancing clinical utility, (c) increasing developmental appropriateness, (d) improving psychometric properties, and (e) increasing user-friendliness. Psychometric properties were improved through the inclusion of norm data of a sample of 2,200 English-speaking U.S. children stratified according to results of the 2000 U.S. Bureau of the Census demographics. Additionally, 550 children from special groups comprising intellectually gifted, mild or moderate mental retardation, learning disabled, ADHD, learning disorder and ADHD, Expressive and Mixed Receptive-Expressive Language, Autism, Asperger's, Traumatic Brain Injury, and Motor Impairment were included to examine WISC-IV utility in small nonrandom samples of children with general diagnostic criteria.

To update the instrument's theoretical foundations, new subtests were introduced to improve the assessment of fluid reasoning, working memory, and processing speed. Fluid reasoning is believed to measure abstraction and concept formation while being relatively free of cultural and educational background. Three new subtests, Word Reasoning, Picture Concepts, and Matrix Reasoning, were included in the WISC-IV to measure this ability. Working memory, the ability to temporarily store information for manipulation, is also suggested to be a component of fluid reasoning; and an additional subtest, Letter-Number Sequencing, was added to the WISC-IV to better assess this area. The measurement of processing speed was improved through the inclusion of a new subtest, Cancellation.

The 10 subtests retained from the WISC-III include: Block Design, Similarities, Digit Span, Coding, Vocabulary, Comprehension, Symbol Search, Picture Completion, Information, and Arithmetic. Three timed subtests, Picture Arrangement, Object Assembly, and Mazes of the WISC-III, were removed from the battery. Two subtests, Arithmetic and Picture Completion were revised and moved into optional status. Arithmetic is now untimed and contains new verbatim instructions and an extended floor and ceiling. Picture Completion includes redrawn pictures, less focus on fine detail, and greater demand for reasoning. Lastly, five new subtests, Picture Concepts, Letter-Number Sequencing, Matrix Reasoning, Word Reasoning, and Cancellation were newly included in the WISC-IV (Flanagan & Harrison, 2005).

Picture concepts. The student is required to choose one picture from each of two or three rows of pictures to form a group with a common characteristic. Picture Concepts measures Induction ability, which is a child's ability to discover the underlying characteristic (e.g., rule, concept, process, trend, class membership) that governs a problem or set of materials.

Letter-number sequencing. The student is presented with a number and letter sequence orally and required to recall numbers in ascending order and letters in alphabetical order. Letter-Number Sequencing requires a child to apprehend and hold information in immediate awareness and to use it within a few seconds. Thus, this subtest measures a child's ability to temporarily store information and perform a set of cognitive operations that require divided attention and the management of the limited capacity of short-term memory.

Matrix reasoning. The student is required to complete a picture matrix by selecting one of five response options that best fits the picture matrix. Matrix Reasoning measures a child's ability to form and recognize concepts, perceive relationships among patterns, and perform deduction (ability to start with stated rules or conditions and to engage in one or more steps to reach a solution to a novel problem) and induction.

Word reasoning. The student is presented with a series of clues and required to identify a common concept being described by the clues. Word Reasoning measures a child's lexical knowledge, which includes the extent of his or her vocabulary that can be understood in terms of correct word meanings.

Cancellation. The student is required to scan random and nonrandom arrangements of pictures and mark target pictures within a time limit. Cancellation measures a child's processing speed, visual selective attention, vigilance, and visual neglect.

The WISC-IV requires the administration of 10 core subtests to obtain the four index scores and the FSIQ. The 10-subtest core battery can be supplemented with one or more of five supplemental subtests. The VCI has one less subtest than the WISC-III and is comprised of Similarities, Vocabulary, and Comprehension, with Word Reasoning and Information being supplemental (optional) subtests. The VCI is a measure of verbal concept formation, verbal reasoning and comprehension, acquired knowledge, and attention to verbal stimuli. The VCI is considered to be a purer measure of verbal reasoning than the VIQ because it measures a narrower domain of cognitive functioning and is less confounded by other areas of functioning (i.e., working memory).

The PRI includes Block Design, Picture Concepts, and Matrix Reasoning, with Picture Completion being a supplementary subtest. The PRI measures fluid reasoning, spatial processing, attentiveness to detail, and visual-motor integration. In contrast to the WISC-III POI, the WISC-IV PRI now has two new untimed motor-free estimates of visual reasoning (Picture Concepts and Matrix Reasoning) and only one timed visual-motor subtests (Block Design) vs. three on the WISC-III. Picture Completion is now a supplementary subtest, and Object Assembly, Picture Arrangement and Mazes have been dropped. It is suggested that the diminished emphasis on fine motor coordination and speed on the PRI may result in a clearer distinction from PSI than was POI on the WISC-III (Flanagan & Harrison, 2005).

The PSI consists of Coding and Symbol Search, with Cancellation as a supplementary subtest. The PSI remained unchanged; however, one new speed-of-processing test (Cancellation) was added as a supplemental subtest. The PSI measures the rapidity with which an individual can process simple or routine information without making errors. Distinguishing between PSI, which includes a graphomotor speed component and the PRI which no longer does, results in an improved recognition of the influence of slowed or impaired visuomotor performance as a contributing factor to a child's functioning. Given the fact that many neurodevelopmental conditions result in deficits in psychomotor speed and written performance, the new ability of the WISC-IV to partition writing speed tasks more effectively and to make reasoning strengths and weaknesses more apparent is seen as an advantage to the WISC-III.

The WMI is comprised of Digit Span and Letter-Number Sequencing, with Arithmetic being a supplementary subtest. The move of Arithmetic to supplementary status in the WISC-IV is suggested to render the WMI factor more sensitive to attention problems than the FDI on the WISC-III because it is no longer confounded by math ability. The WMI measures mental capacity including temporary storage of incoming information, as well as calculation and transformation processing (Flanagan & Harrision, 2005).

An additional change in the WISC-IV is that all four of the WMI and PSI subtests are included in the calculation of the FSIQ, as opposed to only two of the four subtests on the WISC-III. As a result, children with low WMI and PSI scores may gain lower FSIQ scores on the WISC-IV compared to the WISC-III. Particularly, children with ADHD, ADD, LD, autism, and bipolar disorder who show lower performance on these factors likely show lower FSIQs, which makes FSIQ scores an unreliable measure of intelligence for these groups (Hale, Fiorello, Kavanagh, Hoeppner, & Gaither, 2001).

Analysis of Cognitive Abilities

The methods most commonly employed to analyze the cognitive abilities of individuals and groups include scatter, profile, and cluster analyses. This literature review provides a brief overview of the different techniques and then discusses empirical research employing these techniques with gifted and twice-exceptional students.

Scatter analysis is an analysis of the variability of an individual's subtest scores and can be used to determine the difference between the highest and lowest subtests scores or *scatter* on an intelligence test (Kamphaus, Petoskey, & Walters Morgan, 1997). It was long assumed that individuals of average ability had a small amount of scatter of three or four points (a *flat* profile). However, this assumption was found to be erroneous. In a study using the WISC-R norm group of 2200 children, Kaufman (1976) found that the average range of subtest scatter between the highest and lowest scaled scores was 7 points, or more than two standard deviations. There was an average scatter of 4.5 points on the Verbal Scale and a scatter of 5.5 points on the Performance Scale. A study on the subtest scatter of the WISC-III revealed almost identical results. The Verbal Scale revealed an average subtest scatter of 4 points, the Performance Scale 6 points, and the FSIQ 7 points (Sattler, 1992; Wechsler, 1991).

Profile analysis is a practice related to scatter analysis and explores the profile (shape) of an individual's scaled scores. Profile analysis focuses not only on an individual's overall ability score, but also examines the pattern of high and low subtest scores of an individual's profile (Kamphaus et al., 1997). It examines subtest clusters of tests or batteries to identify strengths and weaknesses (Lovett & Lewandowski, 2006). A profile of raw standard scores on a set of variables is obtained for each person or group of persons, and comparisons among profiles are made. The main features of profile analysis include level (mean), dispersion (standard deviation), and shape (range). In its broadest sense, profile analysis could include factor analysis, cluster analysis, and scatter analysis (Cronbach & Gleser, 1953).

Sattler (1988) described the most common methods of profile analysis used on the WISC, including (a) Comparing Verbal and Performance IQs, (b) comparing each Verbal Scale subtest scaled score with the individual's mean Verbal Scale scaled score, (c) comparing each Performance Scale subtest scaled score with the individual's mean Performance Scale scaled score, (d) comparing each subtest scaled score with the mean subtest scaled score based on all subtests administered; (e) comparing sets of individual subtest scores, (f) comparing the index scores, and (g) comparing subtest scaled scores in each index with their respective mean index score. A profile analysis conducted on the WISC may consist of any or all of these approaches.

The ipsative or univariate systematic method of profile analysis examines positive and negative deviations of subtest scores from the individual's own mean to reveal strengths and weaknesses. Thus, the individual is used as his or her own norm base (Glutting, McDermott, Watkins, Kush, & Konold, 1997). The practical purpose of this analysis with the Wechsler scales is to make inferences about strengths and weaknesses, which might aid in making recommendations for treatment and programming. The advantage of ipsative profile analysis is that it reveals a comprehensive view of an individual's abilities by systematically comparing each score to the person's mean scaled score. This guarantees that an individual's strengths and weaknesses will be comparable to his or her own ability level and that significant score differences represent meaningful fluctuations (Kaufman, 1994).

Subtest scores can be compared directly with each other or with the mean of either the verbal or performance scale, depending on which scale the subtest falls. Wechsler (1974) suggested that a difference of three points or more between subtests is significant at the 15% level of confidence and should be examined more closely. Kaufman (1979) recommended comparing each subscale to the child's Verbal and Performance mean score, suggesting that a 3-point difference between a subtest and the child's mean should be viewed as a strength or weakness, respectively. According to Nielsen (2002), a discrepancy of 7 scaled-score points between an individual's highest and lowest subtest score may be suggestive of twice-exceptionality and should be examined further. Several researchers examined the scatter of WISC factor and subtest scores among gifted children as well as twice-exceptional children.

Verbal-Performance IQ Discrepancy

Analysis of the verbal-performance discrepancy of children's IQ tests has been suggested as a means to identify twice-exceptional individuals, as well as to better understand the cognitive behaviors and needs of this population. Several researchers explored the verbal-performance discrepancy among gifted and, to a lesser degree, among twice-exceptional children and adolescents. Research investigating discrepancies between verbal and performance IQ scores in gifted children has typically noted that these children score significantly higher on the Verbal Scale. For example, Silver and Clampit (1990) found verbal IQ scores of 20% of gifted individuals to be 21 or more points higher compared to their performance scores. In addition, the authors suggested that without ceiling effects on several of the subtests, which artificially reduce these individuals' overall scores, discrepancies may have been even more dramatic.

Patchett and Stansfield (1992) examined the Verbal-Performance discrepancy on the WISC-R among children who obtained an IQ score in the range of 120-129 and found that 36% of subjects had a discrepancy of 12 points, while 22% had a discrepancy of 15 points. In a similar study of the WISC-R standardization sample, Kaufman (1976) found that 34% exhibited a Verbal-Performance IQ discrepancy of 12 points, while 25% showed a discrepancy of 15 points or more. In an analysis of the 118 gifted children of the WISC-III standardization sample, Prifitera and Saklofske (1998) found that 54 students exhibited a Verbal-Performance IQ discrepancy of 11 points or greater, while 32 students showed a discrepancy of 16 points.

Researchers comparing the scores on the Verbal and Performance scales of twice-exceptional children on the WISC-R and WISC-III have not found a discrepancy specific to this population, but instead have noted contradictory results. Schiff et al. (1981) noted that twice-exceptional students show higher scores on the verbal cluster of subtests in the Wechsler tests than on the performance subtests. In contrast, Fox (1983) noted that most twice-exceptional students show a higher Performance IQ than Verbal IQ. Lastly, Barton and Starnes (1989) found no significant difference between Verbal and Performance IQ among twice-exceptional students. Due to the contradictory findings of these studies, no conclusions regarding the verbal-performance discrepancy among twice-exceptional students can be drawn; and more research investigating this area is needed.

However, a simple comparison between verbal and performance IQ is viewed as insufficient to draw conclusions about an individual's cognitive abilities because these scores lump together several subtests, leading to the averaging of strengths and weaknesses in both domains in the composite scores. For example, an individual may show high performance on spatial subtests and low performance on Coding, resulting in an average Performance IQ score, which muddles specific information about the individual's cognitive ability. Thus, relying simply on these two scores would conceal more authentic discrepancies that can only be discovered when examining differences between all subtest scores (Baum & Owen, 2004).

Analysis of WISC Factors and Subtests

Due to the limitations of an analysis of verbal-performance discrepancies, the analysis of subtest scores and their combination into factors may be more meaningful to reach a better understanding of the twice-exceptional population. As mentioned previously in the discussion on gifted identification, several researchers particularly recommend the examination of subtest scatter on IQ tests in the identification of twice-exceptional children and adolescents (Brody & Mills, 1997; Nielsen, 2002; Silverman, 2003). Several reasons support the use of an analysis of subtest scores on the WISC as part of the identification of twice-exceptional individuals. For example, because the learning, social-emotional, or behavioral difficulties of these students may dramatically lower the FSIQ scores of this population, many of these students may not qualify for the inclusion in gifted programs, even though they may demonstrate strong gifts in several areas. An analysis of subtest patterns provides a more accurate picture of the conceptual abilities of these students than a total IQ score, which likely underestimates the potential of this population.

In addition, the observation of IQ subtest scores provides crucial information about the strength and weakness patterns common among twice-exceptional children and adolescents, which can largely contribute to the identification and provision of services to this underserved population (Baum & Owen, 2004). According to the American Psychiatric Association (2000), if there is significant scatter among subtest scores on IQ measures, then the analysis of a profile of strengths and weaknesses more accurately reflects an individual's abilities than is the mathematically derived FSIQ. In addition, subtest scores can provide specific information that is lost if analyses are based solely on factor or index scores (Kramer, 1993; Nyden, Billstedt, Hjelmquist, & Gillberg, 2001). According to Kaufman (1994) and Sattler (2002), the WISC subtests have sufficient specificity (i.e., reliability and distinctiveness) to justify subtest analysis.

Gifted students. Research exploring the subtest scatter of gifted individuals on the WISC-R indicated a tendency toward significant subtest scatter (Schiff et al., 1981; Wilkinson, 1993). Patchett and Stansfield (1992) found that subtest scatter increases as IQ scores increase into the superior range. Their research revealed that 20% of individuals with an FSIQ of 110-119 demonstrated a subtest scatter of nine or more points, while 32% of individuals with an IQ score of 130 and above showed a subtest scatter of nine or more points.

Brown and Yakimowski (1987) conducted a factor analysis of the WISC-R subtest pattern of gifted and average ability subjects and found that gifted and high IQ subsamples demonstrated a more complex factor solution than the average ability group. While the average ability group demonstrated the typical two-factor solution of Verbal Ability and Perceptual Organization, a five-factor solution was needed to account for the variance among children with FSIQs of 119 or greater. The high IQ group scored lowest on the subtests Coding and Digit Span and highest on Similarities, Comprehension, Vocabulary, Information, and Block Design.

Because of the frequent WISC-R subtest scatter found among students of high ability, Fishkin et al. (1996) analyzed the subtest pattern of 42 gifted students on the WISC-III to determine if similar subtest variability is evident on the newer version of the WISC. Results revealed that these students demonstrated relative strengths on the Similarities, Comprehension, and Vocabulary subtests and a weakness on Coding and

Symbol Search. The researchers further found that in contrast to the WISC-R, the Block Design subtest was no longer an area of strength for gifted individuals on the WISC-III, but resulted in an average performance. Fishkin et al. hypothesized that this may have been due to the changed scoring requirements on this subtest. In contrast to the WISC-R, the WISC-III rewards bonus scores for swift reaction time; and a fast reaction time is therefore needed for a superior performance on the Block Design subtest on the WISC-III.

Gifted students with learning disabilities. Several researchers attempted to examine the cognitive ability profile of gifted students with learning disabilities through analyses of the scatter of WISC subtests and factors. Schiff et al. (1981) examined the WISC-R profiles of 30 gifted students with learning disabilities, aged 9 to 16 years. Giftedness was identified by an IQ score of 120 or higher on either the performance or verbal scale of the WISC-R. Learning disability was identified by a significant difference between intelligence and achievement in some academic area, yet the deficit area did not have to be below-grade level. Scores were analyzed in terms of verbal-performance discrepancy, subtest scatter, and scatter among Bannatyne's four factors: Verbal Conceptualization, Spatial, Sequencing, and Acquired Knowledge. Students scored 18.6 points higher on the Verbal IQ than on the Performance IQ, which is almost twice the value of 9.7 found in the normal population. This discrepancy was greater than that in any other group of students reported in the literature. Additionally, mean subtest scores ranged from 9.6 on Coding to 16.2 on Similarities. The sample displayed a scaled-score range of 8.3 on the Full Scale, which is one SD above the range of 7.0 found in the normal population. More specifically, 43% of the sample showed scaled-score ranges of

10 or more points, an amount of scatter found less than 15% of the time in the normal population.

Schiff et al. (1981) then analyzed the group's ability pattern based on the three WISC-R factors. Children achieved outstanding scores (95th percentile) on the four Verbal Comprehension subtests (Information, Similarities, Vocabulary, Comprehension), moderate scores (80th percentile) on the five Perceptual Organizations subtests (Picture Completion, Picture Arrangement, Block Design, Object Assembly, Mazes), and average scores (64th percentile) on the Freedom from Distractibility subtests (Arithmetic, Digit Span, Coding). An analysis of scores based on Bannatyne's framework indicated significant differences among the four factors. Students scored highest on Verbal Conceptualization, followed by Acquired Knowledge, followed by Spatial, and lastly the Sequencing factor. Schiff et al. concluded that the twice-exceptional students displayed strengths in verbal conceptualization and acquired knowledge subtests and weaknesses in spatial and sequencing abilities.

In a related study, Fox (1983) examined the WISC-R profiles of 322 gifted students with reading problems, aged 6 to 15 years. Giftedness was identified by IQ scores of 125 or higher on either the verbal or performance scale on the WISC-R. Learning disability was identified through case history information, behavioral observations, reading achievement of at least 2 years below grade level, and evidence of a significant discrepancy between intellectual potential and academic performance. WISC-R subtest scores were organized according to Bannatyne's (1974) recategorization. Results indicated that gifted students with reading disabilities scored highest on conceptual and spatial tasks and lowest on tasks requiring memorization of isolated facts and sequencing (Coding and Digit Span subtests).

In 1988, Barton and Starnes analyzed the WISC-R subtest patterns of 30 gifted students and 41 gifted students with learning disabilities. Results indicated that the verbal-performance discrepancy (V > P) was not unique to gifted students with learning disabilities but was also found among some LD groups. In the examination of gifted students with learning disability subgroups, it was observed that there was little difference in the FSIQ scores of gifted students with mild, moderate, or severe LD. However, gifted students with mild and moderate learning disabilities showed a pattern of V > P, while gifted students with severe LD showed a pattern of P > V. Additional findings showed that both gifted and gifted students with learning disabilities earned their highest scores on the Similarities subtest and their lowest scores on the Coding subtest. An analysis of subtest scatter further indicated that the twice-exceptional group had more scatter on the Verbal scale than the gifted group. Utilizing the Bannatyne cluster analysis to group the subtests indicated a pattern of Verbal Conceptualization > Perceptual Organization > Sequencing for the gifted and LD groups, but not the twice-exceptional group. Barton and Starnes concluded that the discrepancy of subtest scores may be a more sensitive indicator of identifying gifted students with learning disabilities than Verbal-Performance discrepancies. In addition, Barton and Starnes concluded that the twice-exceptional population appears to be heterogeneous.

In a separate study, Starnes et al. (1988) assessed the same group of 41 gifted students with learning disabilities studied by Barton and Starnes (1989) and an additional 80 gifted students. They confirmed low Arithmetic, Coding, Information, and Digit Span subscores that had been reported for the twice-exceptional population in the Schiff et al. (1981) study. In addition, Starnes et al. found that twice-exceptional students, unlike regular LD students, showed strengths on the Verbal Comprehension Index, comprised of the subtests of Information, Similarities, Vocabulary, and Comprehension.

In a similar study, Waldron and Saphire (1990) analyzed the subtest patterns of 14 twice-exceptional students and 17 nondisabled gifted students, aged 8 to 12 years on the WISC-R, using the classification systems of Bannatyne (1974), Kaufman (1975), Rapaport et al. (1946), and Wechsler (1974). This broad-spectrum factor approach was used to determine which factors or subtest groupings might be most effective for intervention and programming. Factor scores were computed by averaging the scores on the corresponding subtests, and a comparison of the performance of the two groups on the factor scores was conducted. Among the twice-exceptional group, two significant differences were noted, indicating that students scored significantly higher on the Reasoning factor (Similarities, Arithmetic, Comprehension) than on the Sequencing (Arithmetic, Digit Span, Coding) factor or on the Organic Brain Syndrome factor (Digit Span, Coding, Block Design). No significant differences were found among the nondisabled gifted group.

Second, Waldron and Saphire (1990) conducted between-group comparisons on the factor scores, which indicated one significant difference. Twice-exceptional students scored 1.6 points lower on the Organic Brain Syndrome factor than the nondisabled gifted group. Third, discrepancies between an individual's own scaled scores were performed by comparing each scaled score to the child's verbal or performance scaled score average. Results indicated that the twice-exceptional group had more of a relative strength, when compared to their overall ability, on the Verbal Conceptualization factor than the control group, while the control group showed greater relative strength on the Reasoning factor than the twice-exceptional group. Fourth, between-group comparisons were made of participants' WISC-R subtest scores. Findings indicated that subtest scatter was significantly greater among the twice-exceptional group, who scored significantly lower on the Digit Span subtest and significantly higher on the Similarities subtest than the control group. Lastly, the rank ordering of WISC-R subtests was compared for the two groups. Rankings were very similar between groups, with Similarities ranking the highest and Coding and Digit Span ranking the lowest in each group. Yet, while rankings of the average subtest scores for the two groups were very similar, the range in the averages was substantially larger in the twice-exceptional group than in the control group.

Baum et al. (1991) examined the WISC subtest patterns of 50 twice-exceptional students (grades four through six). Results revealed that students showed strengths on spatial tasks, as evidenced by high Block Design subtest scores and on tasks that require recognition of patterned sequences and abstract conceptualization, as shown by high Similarities subtest scores. Yet, students showed weaknesses with detailed memory, as evidenced by low Arithmetic subtest scores, with random sequencing, as evidenced by low Digit Span subtest scores, and with processing details as evidenced by low Coding subtest scores (Baum & Owen, 2004).

Dixon (as cited in Baum et al., 1991) hypothesized that the strengths and weaknesses of gifted students with learning disabilities could be clustered in either *integrative* or *dispersive* intelligence. Dixon suggested that gifted students with learning disabilities demonstrate strengths in integrative intelligence, which is related to holistic problem-solving and abstract reasoning, which is necessary for higher level thinking and creative production. Integrative intelligence is assessed by the WISC subtests of Block Design, Object Assembly, Picture Arrangement, Mazes, Similarities, and Comprehension. On the other hand, Dixon hypothesized that dispersive intelligence, which is defined as the ability to remember and use isolated information and learn sequentially from the parts to the whole, is an area of weakness for gifted students with learning disabilities. He suggested that the WISC subtests Vocabulary, Information, Arithmetic, Picture Completion, Coding, and Digit Span assess the area of dispersive intelligence.

Clinical groups. While no studies investigated the cognitive ability of gifted students with behavioral or social-emotional difficulties, several studies investigated the cognitive ability of several clinical groups. Profile analyses of the WISC-III for clinical groups repeatedly demonstrated consistent profiles for these groups. Research indicates that children with ADHD, LD, and autism show weaknesses on the Freedom from Distractibility and Processing Speed Indexes, as well as lower scores on the Coding compared to the Symbol Search subtest (Mayes & Calhoun, 2003; Mayes, Calhoun, & Crowell, 1998; Mealer et al., 1996). Calhoun and Mayes (2005) investigated the WISC-III profiles of 980 children with various clinical disorders including ADHD, ADD, LD, autism, bipolar disorder, anxiety, depression, oppositional defiant disorder, spina bifida, traumatic brain injury, and mental retardation. Results indicated that children with neurological disorders (ADHD, ADD, autism, bipolar disorder, and LD) have lower PSI and FDI than VCI and POI scores, suggesting processing speed, attention, and writing weaknesses. In addition, results revealed that all clinical groups scored lower on the Coding (writing speed) than on the Symbol Search subtest (visual mental speed), which Calhoun and Mayes hypothesized to be due to a writing weakness common among children with clinical disorders. The authors further indicate that their reliable and distinctive findings, consistent with published clinical studies, support profile analysis at both the subtest and factor levels.

Normative Profile Analysis

While researchers generally endorse ipsative profile analysis, several limitations to the approach have been recognized. First, the high incidence of scatter in the normal population has been raised as an objection against this practice. For example, even though a child may present with a significant scatter between subtests, this does not necessarily mean that the discrepancy is diagnostically useful. For example, an examination of the WISC-III standardization sample of 2200 children indicated that 42.7% of these children had one or more subtest scores that were significantly below the child's own mean across subtests (Glutting et al., 1997). A second limitation is the fact that the ipsative method does not determine the uniqueness of a given profile. More specifically, the ipsative approach does not determine whether a profile is commonplace or unique within the general population. A further concern raised about this procedure is that subtests have lower reliability coefficients than the total test score (Lovett & Lewandowski, 2006).

Normative profile analysis is suggested by several researchers to be a method of intellectual profile analysis that is preferred to the ipsative approach. It is a method used by statisticians for comparing individual profiles to the normal population (Glutting,

Konold, McDermott, Kush, & Watkins, 1999). Cluster analyses of the standardization samples of the different WISC scales have revealed normative taxonomies that can be used as normal comparisons when determining the uniqueness of a specific profile. An individual's profile is considered unique when it is established that the profile is not a member of one of the core profile types found in the general population. The researchers endorsing this approach indicate that it is a mathematically superior method in the determination of a typical profile because it compares a particular subtest profile to the profiles common to the standardization sample (Glutting & McDermott, 1990; Glutting et al., 1997).

Robinson and Harrison (2005) examined the WISC-III subtest profiles of 1450 children divided into six sample groups, including children with learning disabilities ($N = 184$), gifted children ($N = 368$), disadvantaged-gifted children ($N = 71$) and gifted children referred but not found eligible for gifted services ($N = 312$). The authors compared the subtest profiles of their samples to the normative taxonomy of eight WISC-III core profiles of the national standardization sample identified by Konold, Glutting, McDermott, Kush, and Watkins (1999). Results indicated that the proportion of students from the six sample groups in the eight core profile categories were significantly different from the proportion found in the WISC-III standardization sample. Findings indicated that several sample groups showed unique profile types that did not fit the eight core profiles of the WISC-III standardization sample. More specifically, 15.8% of students with learning disabilities, 10.3% of gifted students, 21.1% of disadvantaged-gifted students, and 16.7% of students referred but not found eligible for gifted services had unique profiles.

Cluster Analysis

Cluster analysis is a mathematical and statistical method to group participants so that similarities between participants within groups (clusters) are maximized, while simultaneously, similarities between participants from different clusters are reduced (Ward, Ward, Glutting, & Hatt, 1999). Cluster analysis in psychometric evaluation can be viewed as part of profile analysis using its broadest meaning. Sattler (1988), Wechsler (1974), Kaufman (1975) and Bannatyne (1971) used cluster analysis to recategorize WISC-R subtests for the evaluation of learning disabled children. Other researchers cluster analyzed the WISC Scales to identify core profiles present in the general population.

Normative taxonomies. Konold et al. (1999) used multistage cluster analysis to identify profile subtypes based on the 10 core WISC-III subtests within the standardization sample of the WISC-III. This revealed a normative taxonomy of eight core or most typical subtest profiles based on general ability level (FSIQ) and VIQ/PIQ discrepancies. The eight identified core profiles include: High Ability, Above Average Ability, Above Average Ability and VIQ > PIQ, Average Ability and PIQ > VIQ, Below Average Ability and PIQ > VIQ, Below Average Ability, and Low Ability.

Konold et al.'s (1999) High Ability group had a prevalence of 9.1% among the standardization sample with a mean FSIQ of 126.2 and a standard deviation (SD) of 5.5. Mean subtest scores of this ability group are: Picture Completion 13, Information 14, Coding 13, Similarities 14, Picture Arrangement 13, Arithmetic 14, Block Design 15, Vocabulary 14, Object Assembly 14, and Comprehension 14.

Konold et al.'s (1999) Above Average Ability group was found with a prevalence of 14.9% among the standardization sample and demonstrated a mean FSIQ of 113.9 and an SD of 4.4. The subtest pattern of this ability group includes: Picture Completion 13, Information 13, Coding 10, Similarities 12, Picture Arrangement 12, Arithmetic 12, Block Design 12, Vocabulary 12, Object Assembly 12, and Comprehension 12.

Konold et al.'s (1999) Above Average Ability and VIQ > PIQ group showed a prevalence of 10.1% with a mean FSIQ of 108.5 and an SD of 5.2. The mean discrepancy between VIQ and PIQ was found to be 8.5 points in favor of VIQ. The subtest pattern for this group is: Picture Completion 10, Information 12, Coding 13, Similarities 12, Picture Arrangement 10, Arithmetic 12, Block Design 10, Vocabulary 12, Object Assembly 10, and Comprehension 13.

Konold et al.'s (1999) Average Ability and PIQ > VIQ group showed a prevalence of 13.4%, a mean FSIQ of 102.6, and an SD of 5.2. The mean PIQ/VIQ discrepancy was 11.2 points in favor of PIQ. The subtest score pattern of this group includes: Picture Completion 10, Information 9, Coding 13, Similarities 10, Picture Arrangement 12, Arithmetic 10, Block Design 11, Vocabulary 9, Object Assembly 11, and Comprehension 10.

Konold et al.'s (1999) Average Ability and VIQ > PIQ group demonstrated a prevalence of 12.9%, a mean FSIQ of 89.3, and an SD of 4.3. The group showed a mean PIQ/VIQ discrepancy of 6.2 points in favor of VIQ. The group demonstrates the following subtest pattern: Picture Completion 10, Information 11, Coding 8, Similarities 11, Picture Arrangement 9, Arithmetic 10, Block Design 10, Vocabulary 10, Object Assembly 10, and Comprehension 10.

Konold et al.'s (1999) Below Average Ability and PIQ > VIQ group showed a prevalence of 12.9% in the standardization sample, a mean FSIQ of 89.3, and an SD of 4.7. The VIQ/PIQ discrepancy was 10.7 points in favor of the PIQ. The mean score profile for this group is: Picture Completion 9, Information 7, Coding 9, Similarities 7, Picture Arrangement 9, Arithmetic 8, Block Design 10, Vocabulary 7, Object Assembly 10, and Comprehension 7.

Konold et al.'s (1999) Below Average Ability group showed a prevalence of 14%, a mean FSIQ of 87.6, and an SD of 4.8. The subtest pattern for this group includes: Picture Completion 7, Information 8, Coding 9, Similarities 8, Picture Arrangement 8, Arithmetic 8, Block Design 6, Vocabulary 9, Object Assembly 7, and Comprehension 9.

Konold et al.'s (1999) Low Ability group demonstrated a prevalence of 8.4% among the standardization sample, a mean FSIQ of 73.1, and an SD of 6.2. The subtest pattern of this group includes: Picture Completion 6, Information 5, Coding 7, Similarities 5, Picture Arrangement 6, Arithmetic 6, Block Design 5, Vocabulary 5, Object Assembly 6, and Comprehension 6.

Severe IQ differences in the core profile types were determined by cutoff scores, whereby VIQ/PIQ differences of more than 22 points comprise 3% of VIQ > PIQ differences, and VIQ/PIQ differences of more than 24 points comprise 3% of PIQ > VIQ differences. The 3% criterion established by McDermott, Glutting, Jones, and Noonan (1989) approximates differences nearly two SDs above and below the population mean. In accordance with the 3% criterion, it is expected that 3% of children in profile type 3 (Above Average Ability & VIQ > PIQ) exhibit a 22-point VIQ > PIQ difference. Yet, in actuality, 6.3% of children showed a 22-point VIQ > PIQ discrepancy, while no child showed a 24-point PIQ > VIQ discrepancy. A similar outcome was found in profile type 5 (Average Ability & VIQ > PIQ), where instead of the expected 3%, 5.6% of children exhibited a 22-point VIQ > PIQ discrepancy. In contrast, profile types 4 (Average Ability & PIQ > VIQ) and 6 (Below Average Ability & PIQ > VIQ) showed more PIQ > VIQ discrepancies, and profile type 7 (Below Average Ability) had fewer PIQ > VIQ discrepancies.

In a similar study, Donders (1996) conducted a cluster analysis on the standardization sample (2200 children) of the WISC-III to determine core profile subtypes on the basis of the four factor index scores. A two-stage cluster analysis identified five reliable subtypes; three were differentiated based on levels of performance and two based on patterns of performance. The three clusters that were differentiated primarily by level of performance included one cluster that contained below-average scores on all four factor indices, one cluster with a performance of more than one standard deviation above average on all indices, and one cluster with average scores on all indices. Within all clusters, the difference between the highest and lowest average factor score was less than 7 points. The two clusters that were characterized by pattern of performance had PS factor fluctuations as the most prominent source of variance. One cluster obtained average scores on the VC, PO, and FD factors, with PS more than 13 points higher than on any of the other three indices. The second cluster showed a weakness on PS (9-12 points) compared to the other three index scores. Donders indicated that the prominence of the PS factor in the pattern of WISC-III profiles requires further investigation. Possible explanations for reduced processing speed were hypothesized to be due to anxiety, lack of motor coordination, or perfectionistic tendencies. Cluster subtypes did not differ significantly in age, but parental level of education directly covaried with participants' level of performance. While two normative cluster analyses have been conducted with the WISC-III standardization sample, no such analysis has been conducted for the WISC-IV standardization sample at the point of this literature review.

Learning disability profiles. Several studies cluster analyzed the WISC scores of learning disabled individuals and consistently discovered between five and six distinguishable learning disability subtypes. Subtypes typically included one reading or language disabled group, one group with generally depressed abilities, and one group with no observable deficits. Snow, Cohen, and Holliman (1985) examined learning disability subtypes based on the WISC-R subtest scores of 106 public school students identified with learning disabilities. A hierarchical cluster analysis indicated six subtypes with different subtest patterns. Two of these subtypes demonstrated average abilities without any apparent strengths or weaknesses. A third subtype showed consistent below average abilities. A fourth subtype displayed verbal ability deficits. A fifth cluster demonstrated deficits in verbal abilities and generally depressed scores. A sixth and final subtype exhibited low average to average abilities.

In a similar study, Blakely, Crinella, Fisher, Champaigne, and Beck (1994) used key clustering to identify LD subtypes among a sample of 129 identified students with LD and 48 normal students. Subjects were administered a battery including Reitan-Indiana Aphasia Examination, WISC-R, Luria's memory assessment procedure, and Halstead Neuropsychological Test Battery for Children. Results were clustered on six dimensions including general intelligence, balance/coordination, motor strength/speed, tactile/kinesthetic, and communication skills. Six subtypes were identified: (a) low general intelligence and communication skills, (b) low general intelligence but only slightly below normal scores on other dimensions, (c) low motor strength and speed, (d) deficits in auditory verbal memory and language skills, (e) deficits in spatial orientation and conceptualization, and (f) no observable deficits. Blakely et al. concluded that their results support stable subtypes of LD within a neuropsychological context.

Gifted and twice-exceptional subtypes. Cluster analysis investigating WISC subtypes of gifted and twice-exceptional children do not exist at this time. However, due to the heterogeneity of the twice-exceptional population, cluster analysis may be a promising tool in the identification of a typology of twice-exceptionality based on performance on intelligence tests. The identification of twice-exceptional subtypes may increase the understanding of this population and allow the development of more effective identification, classification, and treatment of this group. The use of cluster analysis has recently contributed to the identification of such subtypes in the learning disability field. However, no such studies have been conducted in the gifted or twice-exceptional population. Yet, due to the heterogeneity of this group, such investigations could enhance people's understanding of this often neglected group.

Conclusion

Researchers agree that the assessment of twice-exceptional children and adolescents represents one of the most challenging evaluation situations (Volker et al., 2006). There is a lack of empirical research supporting the current definitions, identification criteria, and interventions employed for twice-exceptional students (Lovett & Lewandowski, 2006). Research investigating characteristics of twice-exceptional students is needed to suggest empirically based definitions, identification criteria, and interventions for this underserved group. Base-rate data on the ability profiles and discrepancies of this population are needed to evaluate the practical significance of scatter and discrepancy cutoffs that have been suggested by previous research. In addition, an exploration of the cognitive ability pattern of twice-exceptional children and adolescents may improve the understanding of this underserved population, facilitate identification, and reduce misdiagnosis among this group.

Research exploring the cognitive processes of twice-exceptional children and adolescents has been limited. While some studies have explored the cognitive abilities of gifted students with learning disabilities, this literature review located no articles on the cognitive ability of gifted students with social-emotional or behavior problems. As a result, this study contributes uniquely to the literature in exploring the WISC profiles of gifted children with behavioral and/or social-emotional difficulties, an area of twice-exceptionality that has been largely neglected by previous research. While the heterogeneity of this population may impede the discovery of specific cognitive patterns present in this group, the diversity of this group indicates the importance of conducting cognitive studies to facilitate the identification as well as the treatment of this population. Cluster analysis is a promising technique that can facilitate the discovery of subtype patterns present among twice-exceptional students.

Examining the subtypes of twice-exceptional children and adolescents can assist in the identification of this group who may otherwise not be recognized, while misdiagnosis may be reduced. In addition, the identification of subtypes of this population provides an understanding of how these students learn best, which can be utilized to create better learning environments for twice-exceptional children and adolescents, as well as to evaluate targeted interventions. Until research projects like the one in this dissertation are completed, the very idea of twice-exceptionality can be criticized as an arbitrary category that is based on a poor psychometric foundation. Thus, this dissertation presents a necessary first step to better understand gifted students with learning, social-emotional, or behavioral difficulties and presents a path toward more focused research questions.

This study began by examining the WISC subtest and factor scatter present among gifted students with learning, behavioral, and social-emotional difficulties. More specifically, the mean scatter among the 11 subtest scores and the four factor indices of the WISC-IV among twice-exceptional students was analyzed. Next, I identified the number of emerging twice-exceptional subtypes when examining WISC-IV subtest scores. This research question was addressed through a cluster analysis of the WISC-IV subtest scores of gifted students with learning, social-emotional, and behavioral problems. Emerging subtypes were not compared to normally occurring profiles, because normative taxonomies have not been identified for the WISC-IV at this time.

CHAPTER 3

METHODS

Participants

Cases to be considered for inclusion in this study were from an archival database of children and adolescents referred to a pediatric neuropsychologist specializing in twice-exceptional individuals. Children and adolescents were mainly referred due to concerns regarding their intellectual, emotional, social, behavioral, and sensory-motor functioning. Participants were administered a broad range of psychological instruments, based on the specific referral question. Participants who met the following criteria were retained for inclusion in the present study: (a) a WISC-IV Full Scale IQ of 120 or higher; and (b) presence of a clinically significant learning disability, behavior problem, or social-emotional difficulty; and (c) age 6 years 0 months to 16 years 11 months.

The final sample consisted of 95 participants (67 males, 28 females) between the ages of 6 and 16 years ($M = 10.29$, $SD = 2.94$). The ethnic background of the sample included: 86.3% White, 8.4% African American, 3.2% Latino, 1.1% Middle Eastern, and 1.1% Other.

Procedures

Participant data were derived from archival cases of neuropsychological evaluations conducted between 2004 and 2008. Measures were individually administered and scored according to standardized procedures by a licensed neuropsychologist. Test scores were obtained within the context of a comprehensive neuropsychological evaluation, which, in addition to the WISC, included several other measures depending on the specific referral question. Twice-exceptionality was assessed through clinical interview, behavioral observation, and the administration of a specific neuropsychological battery depending on the referral question. The battery included several of approximately 65 different measures used to assess the following domains of functioning: Intelligence and Cognitive/Mental Status (6), Achievement (2), Attention and Executive Functioning (8), Memory (7), Auditory Processing and Language (7), Sensory and Motor (13), Personality and Psychopathology (13), Motivation and Malingering (6), and Other (3).

The archival data utilized for this study consisted of the WISC-IV Full Scale IQ, factor index scores, mandatory subtest standard scores, and one supplementary subtest score (Information). Additional supplementary (optional) subtests were not utilized because they were not administered routinely and do not contribute to the computation of the IQ scores. In addition to the WISC-IV scores, demographic information including gender, age, and ethnicity was obtained about each student in the sample. All identifying information was removed to ensure confidentiality.

Measures

The measurement instrument used in this study was the Wechsler Intelligence Scale for Children- Fourth Edition. The Wechsler Intelligence Scale is the most commonly used means for testing intelligence by diagnosticians and other professionals.

The WISC-IV (Wechsler, 2003) is the most recent revision of the WISC. It is an individually administered, comprehensive clinical instrument for assessing the intelligence of children ages 6.0 through 16.11 years. The WISC-IV standardization sample consists of 2200 children stratified by age, sex, race, parent education, and geographic region based on data from the March 2000 U.S. Bureau of Census.

The internal consistency reliability coefficient for the WISC-IV FSIQ was .97 for all ages. The factor index scores, VCI, PRI, WMI, and PSI also have strong internal consistency reliability, with respective coefficients of .94, .92, .92, and .88. The internal consistency of the WISC-IV subtests ranged from .79 to .90, with the majority of subtests in the .80 to .89 range (Wechsler, 2003).

The FSIQ test-retest stability coefficient of the WISC-IV was .89. Average test-retest stability coefficients for the four factor index scores include: .89 for VCI, .85 for PRI, .85 for WMI, and .79 for PSI. The average test-retest stability coefficient for the WISC-IV subtests ranged from .68 to .85 (Wechsler, 2003).

Several studies correlated the WISC-IV with the WISC-III, Wechsler Preschool and Primary Scales of Intelligence- Third Edition (WPPSI-III; Wechsler, 2002), Wechsler Adult Intelligence Scale- Third Edition (WAIS-III; Wechsler, 1997), and Wechsler Abbreviated Scales of Intelligence (WASI; The Psychological Corporation, 1999) to assess the measure's validity. Results indicated correlations of .82 to .89 between the WISC-IV FSIQ and the FISQ scores of the other reported Wechsler Scales. Correlations between the WISC-IV Index scores and the Index scores of the other reported Wechsler Scales ranged from .62 to .85 (Wechsler, 2003).

The predictive validity of the WISC-IV was assessed by comparing the WISC-IV to the Wechsler Individual Achievement Test- Second Edition (WIAT-II; The Psychological Corporation, 2002). Results indicated a correlation between the WISC-IV

FSIQ and the WIAT-II Total achievement score of .87. Correlations between the WISC-IV FSIQ and the WIAT-II Reading, Mathematics, Written Language, and Oral Language composites were .78, .78, .76, and .75 respectively (Wechsler, 2003).

Data Analysis

The present study was conducted in seven steps: First, I examined the performance of the entire sample of twice-exceptional children and adolescents on the WISC-IV via the computation of means, standard deviations, and ranges for the WISC-IV FSIQ, VCI, PRI, WMI, PSI and the 11 subtest scores. I used a one-sample t test to compare the overall factor index score scatter present among the sample to the mean factor index score discrepancy found in the WISC-IV standardization sample. Additionally, I calculated the overall subtest score scatter obtained by the present sample and compared to the subtest score discrepancy found in the WISC-IV standardization sample, using a one-sample t test.

Second, this study aimed to identify the number of twice-exceptional subtypes on the WISC-IV. To address this research question, I submitted WISC-IV FSIQ, factor index, and subtest scores to a hierarchical agglomerative cluster analysis using Ward's (1963) minimum sum of squares method through SPSS (Norusis, 1995). This method is recommended based on research indicating that it is among the best performing hierarchical clustering algorithms and its effective use in previous WISC-III taxonomic research (Donders, 1996; Glutting, McDermott, Prifitera, & McGrath, 1994). I applied Squared Euclidian distance to the data as a similarity measure to estimate the number of clusters present in the sample. This method is recommended due to its sensitivity to the relative level, shape, and pattern of a given profile (Donders, 1996).

Third, I compared the obtained cluster solution on demographic information, including gender, age, and ethnicity. I used Chi-Square tests of independence to compare the different clusters based on gender and ethnicity. I performed a one-way analysis of variance to obtain the effect of mean ages on the different clusters.

Fourth, I obtained descriptive statistics, including mean and standard deviation for the FSIQ and four factor index scores for each of the clusters that were extracted through the hierarchical cluster analysis. Next, I computed factor index score scatter obtained by each of the clusters and compared it to the mean scatter found in the WISC-IV standardization sample through the use of one-sample t tests. In addition, I used paired-samples t tests to determine whether any of the factor index scores obtained by a given cluster differed significantly from any others.

Fifth, I calculated descriptive statistics, including mean and standard deviation for the 11 subtest scores for each of the clusters. I computed subtest score discrepancies and compared them to the mean subtest scatter found in the WISC-IV standardization sample through the use of one-sample t tests.

Sixth, I utilized crosstabulation to obtain the count and percentage of primary and secondary diagnoses present in each cluster.

Seventh, I used a multivariate analysis of variance (MANOVA) to determine whether the different clusters differed from each other on any of the four factor index scores. I used Hotelling's T^2 to assess the statistical significance on the means of the four factor index scores between the different clusters.

CHAPTER 4

RESULTS

The present study examined the WISC-IV profiles of 95 twice-exceptional children and adolescents to facilitate the discovery of subtype patterns present among this group. At first, I examined the factor and subtest scatter among the entire sample of twice-exceptional children and adolescents and compared them to the WISC-IV standardization sample through the use of a one-sample t test. Next, I conducted a cluster analysis on the sample's WISC-IV FSIQ, factor index, and subtest scores to identify the number of emerging twice-exceptional subtypes. I compared the emerging subtypes based on age, gender, and ethnicity using one-way analysis of variance and chi square statistics. In addition, I calculated the count and percentage of primary and secondary diagnoses of the different subtypes using crosstabulation. I utilized paired-sample t tests to determine any significant differences between factor scores within the different subtypes. In addition, I used one-sample t tests to compare the factor and subtest discrepancies obtained by the different cluster subtypes to the scatter found in the standardization sample. Lastly, I conducted a MANOVA to determine if the cluster subtypes differed significantly from each other on the four factor indices.

Descriptive Sample Statistics

I computed means, standard deviations, and ranges for the WISC-IV for the entire group of participants. The means, standard deviations, and ranges for the FSIQ, factor indices, and subtest scores of the WISC-IV for the entire sample are presented in Table 1. As a group, this clinic-referred sample obtained scores within the Superior range on the WISC-IV FSIQ ($M = 122.22$), within the Superior range on the VCI ($M = 127.51$) and PRI ($M = 121.28$), within the High Average range on the WMI ($M = 110.48$), and within the Average range on the PSI ($M = 103.08$). A substantial VCI > PSI discrepancy of 24.43 points and wide fluctuations in the subtest profile were evidenced by a range in mean scaled scores of 9.48 (Coding) to 15.34 (Similarities) within the sample.

I compared the mean VCI > PSI discrepancy of 24.43 points attained by the twice-exceptional sample in the present study to the discrepancy rate obtained by the WISC-IV standardization sample. According to the WISC-IV manual Table B.2., a VCI > PSI discrepancy of 24 points or more occurred in 14.6% of the standardization sample (FSIQ > 120; Wechsler, 2003, p. 262). Further, a VCI > PSI discrepancy of 40 points or more occurred in 2% of the standardization sample (FSIQ > 120; Wechsler, 2003, p. 262), while the same discrepancy occurred in 22.1% of the twice-exceptional sample. Thus, a 40-point discrepancy was approximately 11 times more common in the twice-exceptional sample compared to the standardization sample of children and adolescents with an FSIQ > 120, a statistically significant difference ($t = 10.82; p > .001$). In addition, I compared subtest scatter obtained by the twice-exceptional sample to the amount of scatter required for statistical significance. I compared the 5.86 point Similarities-Coding discrepancy obtained to the WISC-IV manual Table B.3, which

Table 1

WISC-IV Full Scale IQ, Factor Index, and Subtest Scores for the Entire Sample (N = 95)

Area	Mean	SD	Range
Full Scale IQ	122.22	8.51	100-143
Factor Indices			
Verbal Comprehension	127.51	13.14	89-152
Perceptual Reasoning	121.28	10.37	100-143
Working Memory	110.48	13.52	83-146
Processing Speed	103.08	13.68	75-131
Subtest Scores			
Information	14.15	2.70	7-19
Similarities	15.34	2.32	10-22
Vocabulary	14.12	2.63	8-19
Comprehension	13.92	2.97	5-19
Block Design	12.88	2.79	5-19
Picture Concepts	13.19	2.66	6-19
Matrix Reasoning	14.00	2.54	8-19
Letter Number Sequencing	12.42	2.66	4-19
Digit Span	11.52	2.82	6-19
Symbol Search	11.40	2.45	5-18
Coding	9.48	2.85	2-18

Note. Full Scale IQ and Factor Index scores are reported as standard scores, $M = 100$, $SD = 15$. Subtest scores are reported as standard scores, $M = 10$, $SD = 3$.

indicated that a Similarities-Coding discrepancy of 3.23 points is considered to be statistically significant at the .05 level (Wechsler, 2003).

Identification and Validation of a WISC-IV Typology

I utilized a hierarchical agglomerative cluster analysis in the present study to investigate the number of twice-exceptional clusters that would emerge from profiles based upon a frequently used ability instrument. This technique formed a similarity-dissimilarity matrix within which the similarity between each case was described and then gradually built clusters through the use of agglomerative techniques until similar cases were put into the same clusters. I used Squared Euclidean distances as similarity measures due to their high sensitivity to the relative level, shape, and pattern of a given profile (Aldenderfer & Blashfield, 1984). I chose Ward's minimum variance method (Ward, 1963) as the hierarchical agglomerative cluster technique to complete the analysis, as this method was designed to generate clusters that minimize the variance within them and maximize the homogeneity of cases within each group.

I used 16 cognitive variables in the cluster analysis, including the FSIQ, the four factor index scores, and 11 subtest scores (the 10 core subtest scores and Information) of the WISC-IV. Prior to conducting a cluster analysis, the completeness of the data matrix needs to be considered by searching the data for missing cases. For the current data set, no missing variables were present; therefore, no data imputation methods were needed. Because the present sample was thought to be characterized by heterogeneity, outliers were considered part of the target population and retained for further analysis. Cluster analysis of all 95 cases yielded 1 to 10 clusters; and I selected a 7-cluster solution upon an inspection and comparison of corresponding cluster memberships, descriptive statistics, and interrelationships (Huberty, DiStefano, & Kamphaus, 1997). A 7-cluster solution was found to be the most robust and meaningful in terms of clinical relevance and discernibility of clusters. I computed means and standard deviations for the WISC-IV full scale IQ, factor index, and subtest scores of each of the seven clusters. A graphic display of the seven clusters based on factor indices is presented in Figure 1, whereas

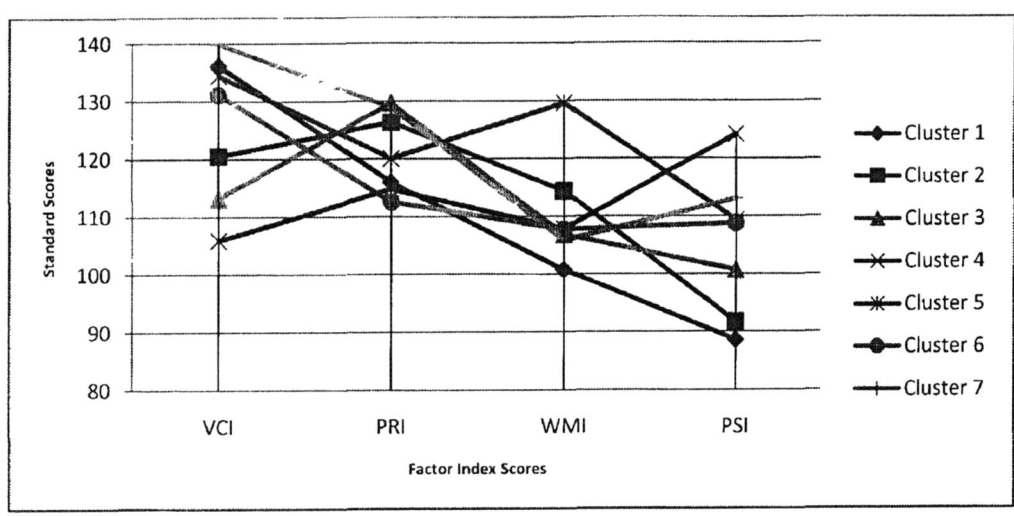

Note. VCI = Verbal Comprehension Index; PRI = Perceptual Reasoning Index; WMI = Working Memory Index; PSI = Processing Speed Index. Factor Index scores are reported as standard scores, $M = 100$, $SD = 15$.

Figure 1. WISC-IV factor index score profiles for the seven WISC-IV cluster subtypes.

Table 2

Mean Full Scale and Factor Index Scores and Standard Deviations for the Seven Cluster Subtypes

Cluster	FSIQ M	SD	VCI M	SD	PRI M	SD	WMI M	SD	PSI M	SD
1	117.44	7.08	136.11	6.31	115.94	10.19	100.67	8.58	88.56	9.43
2	118.73	8.80	120.47	9.05	126.27	8.69	114.33	12.77	91.67	9.40
3	119.15	5.08	113.15	7.05	129.62	3.20	106.77	13.77	100.69	7.66
4	116.50	6.44	105.88	10.30	114.75	8.88	107.75	14.61	124.12	4.09
5	131.47	7.75	134.40	7.75	120.00	11.77	129.60	6.77	109.27	10.32
6	120.69	2.50	131.08	4.87	112.54	5.09	107.69	3.84	108.77	5.12
7	130.31	4.23	139.85	7.00	128.85	6.30	105.77	9.10	113.00	6.89

Note. Population standard scores $M = 100$ and $SD = 15$ for all variables. FSIQ = Full Scale Intelligent Quotient; VCI = Verbal Comprehension Index; PRI = Perceptual Reasoning Index; WMI = Working Memory Index; PSI = Processing Speed Index.

Tables 2 and 3 provide the specific descriptive statistics for the full scale IQ, factor index, and subtest scores.

To validate this cluster solution, I then considered the characteristics of the clusters on other variables that were not included in the clustering process (i.e., gender, ethnicity, and age). No statistically significant differences ($p > .10$) between clusters were found based on gender [$\chi^2(6) = 9.21$, ns] and ethnicity [$\chi^2(18) = 11.18$, ns] (see Table 4). However, a one-way ANOVA performed on the effect of mean ages was significant, [$F(6, 88) = 3.048$, $p = .009$]. Multiple comparisons of each group indicated that the mean age of the participants in Cluster 6 (11.92 years) was significantly higher than the mean age of those in Cluster 4 (7.38 years). Table 5 presents the mean ages for children in the seven clusters. This finding may indicate that children in Cluster 4 may be referred at a younger age, while children in Cluster 6 tend to get referred at a later age. This may suggest that a developmental trend exists in terms of initial referral and diagnosis of a given subtype of twice-exceptional children. Future studies could further examine such developmental trends.

Inspection of Figure 1 and Table 2 indicates that the seven clusters were differentiated primarily by level of performance on VCI, PRI, WMI, and PSI scores. I assigned descriptive labels to the seven clusters based on the most salient features of each profile. As such, the first subtype ($n = 18$) was characterized by a substantial processing speed weakness and a concurrent verbal strength and was, therefore, termed Verbal Learners. Subtype two ($n = 15$) was defined by a processing speed ability in the low end of the average range and was labeled Attention Difficulty. Subtype three ($n = 13$) included children and adolescents with perceptual strengths and was, therefore, termed

Table 3

Mean Subtest Scores and Standard Deviations for the Seven Cluster Subtypes

Variables	1		2		3		4		5		6		7	
	M	SD	M	SD	M	SD	M	SD	M	SD	M	SD	M	SD
IN	15.22	2.10	12.67	1.68	12.15	2.64	11.13	2.90	15.60	2.44	14.62	1.98	16.08	1.71
SI	16.56	1.92	14.47	1.89	12.85	1.57	13.00	1.77	16.53	1.55	15.62	2.22	16.92	1.66
VO	5.56	1.76	12.73	1.87	11.54	1.71	10.62	1.85	15.93	2.25	14.08	1.50	16.38	1.50
CO	15.11	3.51	13.27	2.43	12.62	1.76	9.62	2.72	13.93	1.39	14.85	2.51	16.00	2.48
PCn	12.67	2.22	13.80	2.51	14.92	2.22	11.12	3.14	12.87	3.50	12.54	2.30	13.77	1.70
MR	12.83	2.90	14.87	2.03	15.38	1.90	13.12	1.46	14.33	2.16	12.15	2.70	15.23	2.32
LN	10.83	1.72	13.27	2.76	11.77	3.14	12.00	3.07	15.07	2.63	12.00	1.08	11.92	1.80
DS	9.72	2.08	11.93	2.43	10.92	3.01	11.00	3.12	15.07	2.40	11.15	1.41	10.69	1.84
SS	9.28	1.53	9.73	2.25	10.69	1.55	14.38	2.72	12.40	2.17	12.15	.80	13.23	1.64
CD	6.72	2.24	7.40	1.64	9.38	1.66	14.00	2.51	10.67	2.38	10.77	1.36	10.38	1.94

Note. Population standard scores $M = 10$ and $SD = 3$ for all variables. IN = Information; SI = Similarities; VO = Vocabulary; CO = Comprehension; BD = Block Design; PCn = Picture Concept; MR = Matrix Reasoning; LN = Letter Number Sequencing; DS = Digit Span; SS = Symbol Search; CD = Coding.

Table 4

Frequency of Gender and Ethnicity (Percentage) for the Seven WISC-IV Cluster Subtypes

Variable	1	2	3	4	5	6	7
Gender (%)							
Male	83.3	80.0	46.2	50.0	73.3	61.5	84.6
Female	16.7	20.0	53.8	50.0	26.7	38.5	15.4
Ethnicity (%)							
Caucasian	88.9	86.7	91.7	75.0	80.0	92.3	92.3
African Am.	5.6	13.3	8.3	12.5	6.7	7.7	7.7
Latino	5.6	.0	.0	12.5	6.7	.0	.0
Middle Eastern	.0	.0	.0	.0	6.7	.0	.0

Visual-Spatial Learners. Subtype four (*n* = 8) demonstrated strong processing speed abilities with lower verbal abilities and was called Quick Performers. Subtype five (*n* = 15) consisted of children and adolescents with strong working memory and verbal abilities and was labeled Accelerated Learners. Subtype six (*n* = 13) demonstrated verbal

Table 5

Mean Ages and Ranges in Years for Each Cluster

Cluster	n	M	SD	Range
1	18	10.23	2.49	6-15
2	15	10.87	3.25	7-16
3	13	8.92	2.81	6-13
4	8	7.38	1.51	6-11
5	15	11.00	3.21	7-16
6	13	11.92	2.57	9-16
7	13	10.38	2.66	6-16

strengths with weaker nonverbal abilities and was termed Nonverbal Learning Weakness. Subtype seven ($n = 13$) exhibited verbal and perceptual strengths and was, therefore, called High General Ability. A more thorough description of the seven clusters follows:

Cluster 1: Verbal learners ($n = 18$). This cluster was composed of children and adolescents who had particularly low processing speed abilities, while showing very superior verbal abilities. The subgroup attained WISC-IV factor index scores that were within the Low Average to Very Superior range. The group of Verbal Learners showed the following factor sequence: VCI > PRI > WMI > PSI (see Table 2), with a VCI > PSI discrepancy of 47.55 points. The mean VCI > PSI discrepancy of 47.55 points obtained by the Verbal Learners is more than triple the mean VCI > PSI discrepancy of 12.9 in the normal population ($110 < FSIQ < 119$) and is significantly greater than the normative mean at the .001 level ($t = 10.80$). To determine whether any of the factor scores differed significantly from any others, 95% Bonferroni confidence intervals were used (Morrison, 1976). All comparisons were significant, with findings indicating that children in the group of Verbal Learners scored significantly higher on VCI than on PRI ($t = 10.56; p < 0.001$), significantly higher on VCI than WMI ($t = 18.73; p < 0.001$), significantly higher on VCI than PSI ($t = 14.83, p < 0.001$), significantly higher on PRI than WMI ($t = 8.72, p < .001$), significantly higher on PRI than PSI ($t = 7.48, p < .001$), and significantly higher on WMI than PSI ($t = 3.73, p < .05$). An examination of the subtest scores obtained by the Verbal Learners showed that children in this group scored highest on Similarities (16.56) and lowest on Coding (6.72) subtests, with a range of 9.84 points. The scaled-score range of 9.84 earned by the Verbal Learners is slightly more than one standard deviation above the range of 7.0 for the normal population, a significant difference ($t =$

Table 6

Primary Diagnoses (Count and Percentage) of the Seven Clusters

Diagnosis	1	2	3	4	5	6	7
ADHD	17(94.4%)	15(100%)	7(53.8%)	7(87.5%)	10(66.7%)	9(69.2%)	8(61.5%)
Learning Disorder			3(23.1%)				
Cognitive Disorder			1(7.7%)				
Anxiety Disorder			2(15.4%)	1(12.5%)	3(20.0%)	3(23.1%)	5(38.5%)
ODD					2(13.3%)		
Depression	1(5.6%)						
PDD						1(7.7%)	

Note. ADHD = attention deficit hyperactivity disorder, ODD = oppositional defiant disorder, PDD = pervasive developmental disorder.

3.37; $p < .005$). The majority (94.4%) of children and adolescents in the group of Verbal Learners carried a primary diagnosis of ADHD, while 5.6% had a primary diagnosis of depression (see Table 6). In addition, 44.4% of children in this cluster had a secondary diagnosis, including Learning Disorder, Anxiety Disorder, Oppositional Defiant Disorder, and Pervasive Developmental Disorder (see Table 7).

Table 7

Secondary Diagnoses (Count and Percentage) of the Seven Clusters

Diagnosis	1	2	3	4	5	6	7
Learning Disorder	3(16.6%)	1(6.7%)		4(50%)	1(6.7%)		1(7.7%)
Anxiety Disorder	3(16.6%)	2(13.3%)			1(6.7%)		1(7.7%)
ODD		1(5.6%)	2(15.4%)				
PDD		1(5.6%)			1(6.7%)	1(7.7%)	

Note. ADHD = attention deficit hyperactivity disorder, ODD = oppositional defiant disorder, PDD = pervasive developmental disorder.

Cluster 2: Attention difficulty ($n = 15$). Cluster 2 was composed of children and adolescents who demonstrated processing speed at the very low end of the average range. The Attention Difficulty group obtained WISC-IV factor index scores that were within the Average to Superior range and showed the following factor sequence: PRI > VCI > WMI > PSI (see Table 2), with an overall scatter of 34.60 points. The mean PRI > PSI discrepancy of 34.60 points attained by the Attention Difficulty group is more than double the mean PRI > PSI discrepancy of 12.7 points obtained in the normal population (110 < FSIQ < 119) and is significantly greater than the normative mean at the .001 level ($t = 7.81$). Ninety-five percent Bonferroni confidence intervals were used to determine whether any of the factor scores obtained by the group differed significantly from any others. Findings indicated that children in the Attention Difficulty group scored significantly higher on PRI than on VCI ($t = 2.26$; $p < 0.05$), significantly higher on VCI than PSI ($t = 14.66$; $p < .001$), significantly higher on PRI than WMI ($t = 2.57, p < .05$), significantly higher on PRI than PSI ($t = 12.34, p < .001$), and significantly higher on WMI than PSI ($t = 5.13, p < .001$), while there was no significant difference between VCI and WMI scores. In addition, children in this group scored highest on Matrix Reasoning (14.87) and lowest on Coding (7.40) subtests, obtaining a scatter of 7.47 points, which is only slightly above the mean range of 7.0 for the normal population and does not constitute a significant difference. All children (100%) in the Attention Difficulty group had a diagnosis of ADHD (see Table 6). In addition, 13.3% of children and adolescents in this group exhibited a secondary diagnosis of Anxiety Disorder, while 6.7% had a secondary Learning Disorder (see Table 7).

Cluster 3: Visual-spatial learners ($n = 13$). The third cluster is characterized by children and adolescents with superior perceptual abilities. The subgroup attained WISC-IV factor index scores that were within the Average to Superior range, with the following factor sequence: PRI > VCI > WMI > PSI (see Table 2). The Visual-Spatial Learners displayed a PRI > PSI scatter of 28.93, a discrepancy that is approximately double the value of 12.7 in the normal population and is significantly greater than the normative mean at the .001 level ($t = 9.26$). A comparison of factor scores within the group of Visual-Spatial Learners indicated that the group performed significantly higher on PRI than on VCI ($t = 6.75; p < .001$), significantly higher on VCI than PSI ($t = 3.85, p < .05$), significantly higher on PRI than WMI ($t = 6.42, p < .001$), significantly higher on PRI than PSI ($t = 16.51, p < .001$), and significantly higher on WMI than PSI ($t = 2.26, p < .05$), while there was no significant difference between VCI and WMI scores. In addition, an examination of the subtest scores obtained by the Visual-Spatial Learners indicated that children in this group scored highest on Matrix Reasoning (15.38) and lowest on Coding (9.38) subtests, with a range of 6.0 points, which does not differ significantly from the subtest range of 7 points found in the normal population. Children and adolescents in the group of Visual-Spatial Learners carried primary diagnoses of ADHD, Learning Disorder, Anxiety Disorder, and Cognitive Disorder (see Table 6). Additionally, one individual in this group showed a secondary diagnosis of Oppositional Defiant Disorder (See Table 7).

Cluster 4: Quick performers ($n = 8$). The fourth cluster consists of children and adolescents with superior processing speed and average verbal abilities. Quick Performers showed WISC-IV factor index scores within the Average to Superior range, obtaining the following factor sequence: PSI > PRI > WMI > VCI (see Table 2). The group displayed a PSI > VCI scatter of 18.24, a discrepancy that does not differ significantly from the normative mean (110 < FSIQ < 119) of 11.5. An examination of factor scores within the group of Quick Performers indicated that the group performed significantly higher on PSI than VCI ($t = 5.24, p < .05$), significantly higher on PSI than PRI ($t = 2.51, p < .05$), and significantly higher on PSI than WMI ($t = 2.98, p < .05$), while there was no significant difference between VCI and PRI, VCI and WMI, and PRI and WMI scores. An inspection of the subtest scores obtained by the Quick Performers showed that children in this group scored highest on Symbol Search (14.38) and lowest on Comprehension (9.62) subtests, a discrepancy that does not differ significantly from the standardization sample. The majority of individuals in the Quick Performers group carried a primary diagnosis of ADHD (87.5%), while one individual exhibited a primary Anxiety Disorder (see Table 6). Additionally, half the children and adolescents in this group (50%) had a secondary Learning Disorder (see Table 7).

Cluster 5: Accelerated learners ($n = 15$). The fifth cluster is composed of children and adolescents with superior working memory and very superior verbal abilities. The subgroup attained WISC-IV factor index scores within the Average to Very Superior range, showing the following factor sequence: VCI > WMI > PRI > PSI (see Table 2). The Accelerated Learners group displayed a mean VCI > PSI scatter of 25.13, a discrepancy that is approximately 1.5 times the mean VCI > PSI scatter of 15.7 attained in the normal population (FSIQ > 120) and is significantly greater than the normative mean ($t = 2.54; p < .05$). A comparison of factor scores within the group of Accelerated Learners indicated that these children and adolescents performed significantly higher on

VCI than PRI ($t = 3.98; p = .001$), significantly higher on VCI than PSI ($t = 6.77, p < .001$), significantly higher on WMI than PRI ($t = 3.24, p < .05$), significantly higher on PRI than PSI ($t = 4.57, p < .001$), and significantly higher on WMI than PSI ($t = 6.71, p < .001$), while there was no significant difference between VCI and WMI scores. In addition, an examination of the subtest scores attained by the Accelerated Learners indicated that children and adolescents in this group scored highest on Similarities (16.53) and lowest on Coding (10.67) subtests, with a range of 5.86 points, which does not differ significantly from the mean subtest scatter range of 7.0 points obtained by the normal population. The group of Accelerated Learners included primary diagnoses of ADHD, Anxiety Disorder, and ODD (see Table 6). The group additionally showed secondary diagnoses in the areas of Learning Disorder, Anxiety Disorder, and Pervasive Developmental Disorder (see Table 7).

Cluster 6: Nonverbal learning weakness ($n = 13$). The sixth cluster includes children and adolescents with very superior verbal abilities. This subgroup obtained WISC-IV factor index scores within the Average to Very Superior range and showed the following factor sequence: VCI > PRI > PSI > WMI (see Table 2). The Nonverbal Learning Weakness group displayed a VCI > WMI scatter of 23.39 points, a discrepancy that is about 1.5 times the value of 13.9 in the normal population (FSIQ > 120) and is significantly greater than the normative mean at the .001 level ($t = 4.53$). An examination of factor scores within the Nonverbal Learning Weakness group indicated that the group scored significantly higher on VCI than PRI ($t = 9.31; p < .001$), significantly higher on VCI than WMI ($t = 11.16, p < .001$), significantly higher on VCI than PSI ($t = 9.03, p < .001$), and significantly higher on PRI than WMI ($t = 2.69, p < .05$), while there was no significant difference between PRI and PSI, and WMI and PSI scores. Further, an inspection of subtest scores attained by the Nonverbal Learning Weakness group indicated that children and adolescents in this group scored highest on Comprehension (14.85) and lowest on Coding (10.77) subtests, with a range of 4.08 points, which is about one standard deviation below the mean range of 7.0 for the normal population, a significant difference ($t = -3.67; p < .05$). The Nonverbal Learning Weakness group included 69.2% of children and adolescents who carried a primary diagnosis of ADHD, while 23.1% carried a primary Anxiety Disorder, and 7.7% had a Pervasive Developmental Disorder (see Table 6). Moreover, one individual carried a secondary diagnosis of Pervasive Developmental Disorder (see Table 7).

Cluster 7: High general ability ($n = 13$). The seventh cluster is composed of children and adolescents with specific verbal and perceptual strengths. The High General Ability group earned WISC-IV factor index scores within the Average to Very Superior range, displaying the following factor sequence: VCI > PRI > PSI > WMI (see Table 2). The High General Ability group displayed a VCI > WMI scatter of 34.08 points, a discrepancy that is almost 2.5 times the value of 13.9 in the normal population and is significantly greater than the normative mean ($t = 8.27; p < .001$). An examination of factor index scores within the group indicated that all comparisons were statistically significant. Children and adolescents in the High General Ability group scored significantly higher on VCI than PRI ($t = 4.23; p = .001$), significantly higher on VCI than WMI ($t = 13.97; p < 0.001$), significantly higher on VCI than PSI ($t = 8.00, p < .001$), significantly higher on PRI than WMI ($t = 6.42, p < .001$), significantly higher on PRI than PSI ($t = 6.77, p < .001$), and significantly higher on PSI than WMI ($t = 2.23, p <$

.05). Moreover, an examination of subtest scores attained by the High General Ability group indicated that children and adolescents in this group scored highest on Similarities (16.92) and lowest on Coding (10.38) subtests, with a range of 6.54 points, which does not differ significantly from the mean subtest range of 7.0 obtained by the normal population. Children and adolescents in the High General Ability group had primary diagnoses of ADHD and Anxiety Disorder (see Table 6). Moreover, secondary diagnoses of Learning Disorder and Anxiety Disorder were present (see Table 7).

I made comparisons through a MANOVA to determine whether the seven subtypes differed from each other on any of the factor index scores. I used Hotelling's T^2 to assess the statistical significance on the means of the four indices between the seven subtypes. Results from the MANOVA revealed significant differences between the subtypes [$F(24, 334) = 21.35, p < .001$]. Post hoc comparisons indicated that on the VCI, the Verbal Learners subtype obtained a significantly higher score relative to the Attention Difficulty, Visual-Spatial Learners, and Quick Performers subtypes ($p < .001$). The Attention Difficulty subtype showed a significantly higher score on VCI than the Quick Performers while obtaining lower scores on VCI than the Accelerated Learners, the Nonverbal Learning Weakness, and the High General Ability subtypes ($p < .01$). The Visual-Spatial Learners subtype demonstrated significantly lower scores on VCI than Accelerated Learners, the Nonverbal Learning Weakness, and the High General Ability subtypes ($p < .001$). The Quick Performers subtype showed significantly lower scores on VCI than the Accelerated Learners, the Nonverbal Learning Weakness, and the High General Ability subtypes ($p < .001$).

On the PRI index, the Verbal Learners subtype showed significantly lower scores than the Attention Difficulty, the Visual-Spatial Learners, and the High General Ability subtypes ($p < .05$). The Attention Difficulty subtype demonstrated significantly higher scores on PRI than the Quick Performers and the Nonverbal Learning Weakness subtypes ($p < .05$). The Visual-Spatial Learners showed significantly higher scores on PRI than Quick Performers and the Nonverbal Learning Weakness subtypes ($p < .05$). The Quick Performers obtained a significantly higher PRI score than the High General Ability subtype ($p < .05$). The Nonverbal Learning Weakness subtype showed a significantly lower PRI score than the High General Ability subtype ($p < .001$).

On the WMI, the Accelerated Learners subtype obtained significantly higher scores than all other groups ($p < .005$). In addition, the Attention Difficulty subtype scored significantly higher on WMI than the Verbal Learners ($p = .005$).

On the PSI, the Verbal Learners scored significantly lower than the Visual-Spatial Learners, the Quick Performers, the Accelerated Learners, the Nonverbal Learning Weakness and the High General Ability subtypes ($p < .005$), while there was no significant difference to the Attention Difficulty subtype. The Attention Difficulty subtype showed significantly lower scores on PSI than the Quick Performers, the Accelerated Learners, the Nonverbal Learning Weakness, and the High General Ability subtypes ($p < .001$). The Visual-Spatial Learners subtype scored significantly lower on PSI than the Quick Performers and the High General Ability subtypes ($p < .005$). The Quick Performers showed a significantly higher PSI than the Nonverbal Learning Weakness subtype ($p = .002$).

CHAPTER 5

DISCUSSION

The purpose of this study was to identify the cognitive pattern of twice-exceptional children and adolescents to reveal the pattern of abilities present in this heterogeneous group. The WISC-IV full-scale IQ, factor index, and subtest score patterns of twice-exceptional students were identified and validated. A cluster analysis on the entire sample of twice-exceptional students confirmed the heterogeneity of this group, indicating seven reliable subtypes that were differentiated primarily by level of performance on the four factor index scores. These were: (a) Verbal Learners, (b) Attention Difficulty, (c) Visual-Spatial Learners, (d) Quick Performers, (e) Accelerated Learners, (f) Nonverbal Learning Weakness, and (g) High General Ability.

The overall sample of twice-exceptional children and adolescents assessed in this study obtained a factor score sequence of VCI > PRI > WMI > and PSI, which is consistent with the factor sequence observed in the WISC-IV validity study of gifted children (Wechsler, 2003). Gifted students in the validity study showed the following mean factor index profile: VCI = 124.7, PRI = 120.4, WMI = 112.5 and PSI = 110.6. Overall, the sample of twice-exceptional children and adolescents in this study performed within the Superior range on VCI (127.51) and PRI (121.28), while scoring in the High Average range on the WMI (110.48) and within the Average range on the PSI (103.08). The sample displayed a substantial mean VCI > PSI discrepancy of 24.43 points; and

22.1% of the sample demonstrated a VCI > PSI discrepancy of 40 points or more, a scatter obtained by only 2% of individuals in the WISC-IV standardization sample who displayed an FSIQ of 120 or higher. This highlights that the twice-exceptional group exhibited a factor index score discrepancy which is significant and unusual in the normal population.

Overall, the sample of twice-exceptional children and adolescents showed strengths on VCI and PRI compared to lower WMI and PSI scores, which is consistent with research findings on the strengths and weaknesses of gifted children without disabilities (Wechsler, 2003). It has been argued that the two larger VCI and PRI factors are more psychometrically robust, have stronger construct validity, and are more g loaded than the WMI and PSI factors (Flanagan & Kaufman, 2004). The VCI reflects Crystallized Ability, which refers to the breadth and depth of an individual's primarily verbal or language-based acquired knowledge as well as the ability to effectively apply this knowledge. The PRI reflects Visual Processing and Fluid Reasoning. Visual Processing refers to an individual's ability to generate, perceive, analyze, synthesize, store, retrieve, manipulate, transform, and think with visual patterns and stimuli. Fluid Reasoning includes the ability to use mental operations when faced with relatively novel tasks that cannot be performed automatically.

The overall PSI weakness observed in this sample of twice-exceptional children and adolescents is consistent with a PSI weakness among gifted students that has been noted in previous research. For example, the validity studies of the WISC-III and WISC-IV with gifted children both indicated that this group performed lowest on PSI (Wechsler, 1991, 2003). In addition, the twice-exceptional group as a whole showed strengths and weaknesses in the same subtests noted for the gifted population. The twice-exceptional sample scored highest on the Similarities subtest (15.34), which is consistent with research on gifted students without disability, highlighting that gifted students perform highest on Similarities (Fishkin et al., 1996; Wilkinson, 1993). Moreover, the finding that this sample of twice-exceptional students performed lowest on the subtests Coding (9.48) and Symbol Search (11.40) is consistent with previous research indicating that these subtests are frequently weaknesses for gifted individuals, with Coding being the lowest score for gifted children (Brown & Yakimowski, 1987; Fishkin et al., 1996; Patchett & Stanfield, 1992; Wilkinson, 1993). Moreover, Coding and Digit Span subtests have been strong indicators of deficit areas for twice-exceptional students in previous research (Barton & Starnes, 1989; Fox, 1983; Silverman, 1989; Waldron & Saphire, 1990).

The PSI and WMI weaknesses found in this sample of twice-exceptional students are consistent with previous research indicating that children with neurological disorders (ADHD, ADD, autism, bipolar disorder, and LD) show weaknesses on PSI and FDI on the WISC-III compared to their performance on VCI and POI (Calhoun & Mayes, 2005). This suggests that individuals with these diagnoses likely display processing speed, attention, and writing weaknesses. It is important for psychologists to recognize the coexistence of these problems to ensure proper assessment and provision of appropriate interventions for these areas. In addition, because in the WISC-IV all four of the WMI and PSI subtests are included in the calculation of the FSIQ compared to only two of the four FDI and PSI subtests on the WISC-III, children with WMI and PSI weaknesses likely obtain a lower FSIQ on the WISC-IV than on the WISC-III. Thus, particularly for twice-exceptional children with ADHD, ADD, LD, autism, and bipolar disorder, which all tend to negatively affect PSI and WMI, FSIQ may be a particularly unreliable measure of intelligence. Instead, the intellectual ability of these subgroups may be better understood through an inspection of the VCI and PRI scores of these groups.

Kaufman (1994) suggested that PSI is adversely affected by fine-motor problems. That all twice-exceptional subtypes in the present study showed lower subtest scores on Coding (writing speed) than on Symbol Search (visual mental speed) supports this view and suggests that low PSI is likely a consequence of writing weakness. Based on the slower performance speed of twice-exceptional children and adolescents, it is important that the effect of this weakness on overall IQ scores is considered when making interpretations about the overall cognitive ability of this group. A relative weakness in Processing Speed has direct bearing on the interpretation of the FSIQ, because both Coding and Symbol Search subtests are used in the calculation of FSIQ scores.

In addition, time bonuses given on the Block Design subtest can have a significant effect on an individual's PRI and FSIQ scores. Particularly as a child gets older, time bonuses are essential to obtain an Above Average performance on the Block Design subtest. For example, without time bonuses, children 8 years and older are unable to achieve a Block Design score of 2 *SDs* above the mean, while children ages 11 years or older cannot obtain a Block Design score above the average range without time bonuses. Consequently, slow processing speed needs to be considered when interpreting the Block Design and PRI scores of these students. A Block Design No Time Bonus score is available to aid in the interpretation of the score and to determine whether speed of performance significantly impacted a child's performance on this subtest. In addition, testing a child's limits on time-laden tests may further help the examiner to assess a child's accuracy and problem-solving skills without the confound of processing speed (Flanagan & Kaufman, 2004).

The significant scatter present among factor index and subtest scores of twice-exceptional students found in this study continues to highlight the importance of inspecting the profile of strengths and weaknesses of this group, rather than relying on the mathematically derived full scale IQ score. To obtain a true understanding of twice-exceptional students, their discrete sets of abilities need to be analyzed separately rather than averaged into a misleading full scale IQ score. However, because placement in programs frequently continues to be dependent on Full Scale IQ scores, many twice-exceptional students with uneven patterns are denied differentiated programming due to an averaging of extremely discrepant scores. To address this problem, an inspection of ability patterns is highly recommended to better serve this population. Performance on subtest and factor scores on the WISC-IV provides valuable diagnostic information that has clinical and instructional implications.

Cluster Subtypes

Cluster 1

Cluster 1 was termed Verbal Learner and included 18 children and adolescents. This cluster was characterized by processing speed abilities at the low end of the average range (PSI = 88.56), while demonstrating very superior verbal abilities (VCI = 136.11). The Verbal Learner subtype demonstrated the largest factor scatter among all clusters with a VCI > PSI discrepancy of 47.55 points, which is more than triple the mean VCI > PSI scatter found in the normal population. Moreover, significant discrepancies were found among all four factor index scores, with the following factor sequence VCI > PRI > WMI > PSI.

The group's significantly higher (over 1 SD) language/verbal abilities (VCI) compared to their visual processing abilities (PRI) has a number of implications for their overall thinking style and emotional well-being. In general, these children and adolescents process, learn, and perform best with oral language. Thus, this group shows strengths in the processing of words and language-based meanings; listening to, keeping pace with, and following verbal sequences; processing verbal meanings and implications; and simultaneously formulating verbal responses. However, when presented with visual information, Verbal Learners require more time and cognitive resources to complete the steps from input to output of information and may favor language-based meanings. For example, given a verbal/language-based message (e.g., a rule) that conflicts with a visual message such as a social situation that clearly exemplifies an exception to the rule (without being explicitly stated), this group may stick with the rule and be slow to adjust to the contextual (visual) information. In addition, children and adolescents with strong verbal and weak visual abilities also tend toward linear, concrete, and detail thinking vs. non-linear, abstract, and gist thinking. In other words, children and adolescents in this subtype are likely to do better with thinking that involves following the steps, learning the facts, or understanding the particulars/clarifying the details vs. thinking that involves varied approaches, learning about contingencies and possibilities, or understanding the whole or the gist. In the real world, this can play out in a problematic way if a focus on facts and particulars precludes an understanding of the main idea or an appreciation for the importance of context. Thus, Verbal Learners may display difficulties making the implicit explicit and may show a tendency to follow exact rules or guidelines, while lacking the ability to *think outside the box.*

While the VCI-PRI discrepancy present in this subtype has several implications for this group, the group's comparably low processing speed ability makes their profile particularly problematic. Based on their PSI weakness, these students demonstrate visual and motor difficulties, such as poor fine-motor skills and difficulties with hand-eye coordination that likely affect their performance in several areas, including writing and math. Thus, the slow speed of these students is likely experienced as a handicap by them, which can cause frustration and lead to reduced self-esteem. For example, while Verbal Learners have excellent verbal abilities and the conceptual thinking skills required to write outstanding reports, this ability is hindered by the students' struggle with handwriting, fine-motor skills, and slow speed. The wide discrepancy between strengths and weaknesses of this group is likely to cause frustration and interfere with the full development of these children and adolescents. This frustration experienced due to disparate abilities can lead to depression and to an avoidance of growth opportunities including risking failure, setting standards for their work, and setting or meeting goals.

To reduce frustration among this group, it is important that these children and adolescents receive adequate praise and support for their writing efforts to make them more tolerant of their slow speed. Additionally, to address the deficit of this group, providing these students with alternate ways to express ideas and create products must be provided. One avenue that can help this group become more successful learners is using technology to address their weaknesses. For example, students who struggle with processing speed might be allowed to tape-record lectures and may benefit from untimed or oral tests to accommodate their weakness. Additional accommodations utilizing technologies include calculators, hand-held spell checkers, video and digital cameras, computers, voice-activated word processing software programs, computer software that emphasizes critical and creative thinking, and tape-recorded books (Nielsen, 2002). The use of technology can enable Verbal Learners to become more successful learners by accessing and organizing information and improving the visual quality of their finished products.

Cluster 2

Cluster 2 was termed Attention Difficulty and included 15 children and adolescents. Individuals in this subtype performed highest on PRI (126.27) and lowest on PSI (91.57), with the following factor sequence: PRI > VCI > WMI > PSI. Children and adolescents in the Attention Difficulty cluster demonstrate less factor scatter, with the exception of PSI, which was a relative weakness for this group. With the exception of PSI, the factor profile of this subtype shows less scatter (PRI-VCI = 11.94 points), suggesting that individuals in this group are quite capable and likely demonstrate less concurrent frustration, mood, and self-esteem problems than students in Cluster 1. If mood or self-esteem problems are experienced by this group, then such problems are likely to be less intense and impacting.

While the Attention Difficulty subtype is likely to generally perform well in the classroom, individuals in Cluster 2 show difficulties with processing speed. Processing speed requires little complex thinking or mental processing, but instead includes simple, clerical type tasks. These students may struggle with their ability to fluently and automatically perform cognitive tasks, especially when under pressure to maintain focused attention and concentration. Individuals with low processing speed likely struggle with rate of learning, comprehension of new information, speed of performance, and mental fatigue (Prifitera & Saklofske, 1998). Based on their PSI weakness, this subtype would benefit from the accommodations previously mentioned for Cluster 1 to address their processing speed difficulty.

It is noteworthy that all individuals in the Attention Difficulty subtype carried a primary diagnosis of ADHD, which has further implications for this group of students. According to the low arousal theory, individuals with ADHD suffer from a state of abnormally low arousal. Because of their low arousal threshold, students with ADHD are constantly seeking stimulation; and without enough stimulation coming from the environment, ADHD children will engage in self-stimulation, such as fidgeting, talking, or walking around. In addition, the theory holds that individuals with ADHD cannot self-moderate; and their attention can only be sustained by strong environmental stimulation. It is therefore difficult for the person with ADHD to sustain his or her attention on any task of waning stimulation or novelty. This explains why many gifted students who carry a diagnosis of ADHD are highly focused when engaged in areas of strength and interest (i.e., experienced as highly stimulating) while struggling to maintain focus on activities that are experienced as boring or repetitive (Baum et al., 1995). To support these students' ability to sustain attention, it is recommended that educators develop curricula that are engaging for twice-exceptional children with ADHD. This can be accomplished by utilizing an interest-based curriculum or creating entry points to curriculum based on a student's unique profile of talents (Gardner, 1999). Using entry points that match students' strengths and interests can be helpful in more fully engaging the Attention Difficulty student in the curriculum and instruction.

In addition, several school accommodations might be helpful to address attention problems in twice-exceptional children, including preferential seating near the teacher, dividing tasks into more manageable segments, teaching organizational and study skills, allowing two sets of textbooks (one for home and one for school), and backpack check before school and at the end of the school day to ensure that the student does not forget assignments and materials (Barkley, 1994). Also, many of the children in the Attention Difficulty subtype may be very energetic and have difficulty sitting still for sustained periods of time. Allowing these students a *walking corridor* in the back of the classroom where they can stand up and move around a little has been suggested as an appropriate accommodation (Mooney & Cole, 2000). Also, allowing highly distractible students to privately listen to music through headphones can increase their attention by superseding distracting extraneous noises. Other students may benefit from a quiet corner in the classroom that limits both visual and auditory stimulation and allows them to focus on the task at hand.

Moreover, gifted children and adolescents with attention-deficit disorder with or without hyperactivity are at risk for social and emotional adjustment problems. These students may struggle from misidentification, emotional immaturity, peer rejection, family stress, and school stress, difficulties that are enhanced by their struggles with attention and organization (Moon, 2002). Thus, counseling and other strategies addressing the social-emotional problems of this group are recommended and can be found in the clinical implication section of this study.

Cluster 3

Cluster 3 was termed Visual-Spatial Learners and included 13 children and adolescents who were characterized by perceptual abilities in the very superior range (PRI = 129.62). These children and adolescents show a strong ability on tasks that require visual perception, organization, and reasoning with visually presented, nonverbal material to solve problems that are not typically taught in school. Visual-Spatial Learners show a strength in using mental operations when being faced with a novel task that cannot be performed automatically, such as forming and recognizing concepts, perceiving relationships among patterns, drawing inferences, and problem-solving. Cluster 3 includes children and adolescents who might be described as unique, curious, and relationally well-connected. Visual-Spatial Learners are likely experienced as being idiosyncratic, out-of-the box type children, who give interesting answers and have a tendency to make off-the-wall comments.

Based on their lower VCI (113.15) vs. PRI (129.62) score, Visual-Spatial Learners may tend to understand overall concepts but may struggle with their articulation. Also, these individuals may tend to be too abstract and have difficulty verbally articulating the heart of the matter, saying something idiosyncratic rather than addressing the core. These students can best be described as *visual-spatial learners* who think in pictures rather than words. They tend to see the big picture but may miss the details. Their learning occurs in a holistic all-or-none-fashion rather than in the typical step-by-step manner in which most teachers teach. Visual-Spatial Learners struggle to organize information sequentially, which may affect their ability to receive, process, and communicate information. Thus, when taking notes during lectures, this group may become confused as to how to organize the content into major topics and subtopics. Instead of seeing things sequentially, these students are holistic learners and may struggle with more linear tasks, such as writing an essay or developing an outline (Barton & Starnes, 1988). Visual organizers such as webs, Venn diagrams, and storyboards might be particularly helpful to Visual-Spatial Learners. Individuals in this subtype may have a photographic visual memory, which enables them to recall the places they have been and how to get to them. These children and adolescents commonly enjoy doing advanced puzzles, constructing with Legos, completing mazes, playing chess, designing scientific experiments, taking things apart to see how they operate, and playing Tetris on the computer. These students are often gifted creatively, technologically, mathematically, or emotionally.

Students in this subtype might have more learning problems because of the overemphasis on lecturing, rote memorization, as well as drill and practice exercises of traditional academic subjects that focus heavily on verbal abilities. Instead, learning in these students typically occurs all at once, with large chunks of information grasped in intuitive leaps, rather than in gradual accretion of isolated facts. Visual-Spatial Learners thrive on abstract concepts, complex ideas, inductive learning strategies, holistic methods, and activities requiring synthesis. Strategies that are particularly helpful in teaching students with visual-spatial strengths include: using visual aids, such as overhead projectors, and visual imagery in lectures; using manipulative material to allow hands-on experience; using a sight approach to reading rather than phonics; using a visualization approach to spelling; encouraging the discovery of the student's own method of problem-solving; avoiding rote memorization and instead using more conceptual or inductive approaches; avoiding drill and repetition; emphasizing creativity, imagination, new insights, and new approaches rather than the acquisition of knowledge; engaging students in independent studies or group projects that involve problem-finding as well as problem-solving; allowing them to construct, draw, or otherwise create visual representations of concepts; and using computers so that information is presented visually (Silverman, 1989).

Cluster 4

Cluster 4 was termed Quick Performers and included eight students. This subtype was differentiated primarily by a relative strength on the PSI (PSI = 124.12). This indicates that twice-exceptional children and adolescents in this subgroup perform at high speed, while paying attention to detail. More specifically, Quick Performers demonstrate strengths in performing somewhat boring clerical type tasks faster. However, some of their skills, particularly language-based abilities, are actually less well developed. Based on their relatively low scores on VCI (105.88) and their average to high average scores on WMI (107.75) and PRI (114.76), it may be questionable whether this group meets qualifications for giftedness in a more traditional sense. Based on their score profile, this group of children and adolescents shows lower complexity of thoughts, problem-solving ability, and ability to integrate more complex information.

Given that all individuals in this subtype suffered from either ADHD (seven individuals) or Anxiety Disorder (one individual), it is possible that the high PSI score found in this group is coupled with impulsivity. Thus, these children and adolescents may have a tendency to move very fast out of their impulsivity. Consequently, their propensity for tasks that require speed may not necessarily be a strength, because it may lead to less focus on details and mistakes. Similarly, for the individual suffering from an anxiety diagnosis, the high PSI score may be driven by anxiety, causing the individual to be more hypervigilant and engaging in tasks with heightened speed.

While Quick Performers demonstrate Processing Speed strengths, individuals in this group tend to struggle with verbal communication and working memory. To address the weaknesses of this group, visual and kinesthetic experiences used to convey abstract ideas may be helpful. This accommodation removes the stumbling block of verbal communication and allows the visual image to guide the mental processes. Thus, graphics or visuals can allow that abstract ideas are seen rather than heard, bypassing a focus on language. Additional accommodations might include reducing and simplifying verbal input, emphasizing key words, and asking students to repeat and explain instructions.

To address the working memory weakness of this group, accommodations should focus on teaching these students how to invent mnemonics or funny ways to remember small details that are so easily lost among this group. Mnemonic strategies or memory aids are particularly helpful if the student invents his or her personal and original mnemonic (Baum & Owen, 2004). In addition, students may more easily remember material that was acquired in an experiential way, such as through an experiment they conducted or a simulation in which they participated.

Cluster 5

Cluster 5 was termed Accelerated Learners and includes 15 children and adolescents with strong working memory (WMI = 129.60) and verbal (VCI = 134.40) abilities. These students show strong abilities utilizing verbal information and have a well-developed ability to apprehend and hold information in immediate awareness. This group easily learns information, particularly when presented orally and based on their working memory capacity, has little difficulty holding onto facts. Individuals with strong working memory, which has been labeled the *door to learning*, have a tendency to easily acquire new information, integrate it with previously learned facts, and then move it into storage. Accelerated Learners easily follow verbal or written directions, process auditory information, organize thoughts for speaking and writing, and learn multi-step procedures.

Accelerated Learners tend to have sharper attention and filtering capacities in their sensory storage, which allows them to hold accurate images of incoming environmental stimuli. Information is held long enough to sort through it and determine whether or not it merits keeping. While unnecessary information is dismissed, worthwhile data is passed on to long-term storage. This sorting occurs by encoding or interpreting the images of environmental stimuli received by the brain. The group's strong encoding skills in working memory further promote more efficient access routes to information stored in long-term memory. In particular, Accelerated Learners may have large storehouses of personally meaningful information that is placed along well-constructed scaffolding, with clear routes from certain information to other information. Moreover, this group may further demonstrate an ability to rapidly erect new scaffolding, particularly along unpredictable routes.

Due to their strong working memory skills, Accelerated Learners may particularly excel in math, reading comprehension, complex problem-solving and test-taking because they can retain information and prioritize the steps to solving problems. Their strong working memory allows these students to focus intently during tests and to recall the essential information. In combination with their strong verbal skills, Accelerated Learners easily acquire and store new information, particularly if presented orally or in writing. Considering that academic demands are largely reliant on these two pathways of learning, these students often excel in the classroom.

While Accelerated Learners demonstrate a relatively evenly developed profile, they performed somewhat lower on processing speed. Thus, this group of students demonstrates a relative PSI weakness, which might be exhibited by motor difficulties and hand-eye coordination weakness. However, while this group demonstrates a relative PSI weakness, index score scatter is in the *average* range and is therefore likely experienced as less debilitating. Based on the fairly evenly developed profile of this group, these students likely experience less frustration and can find a state of *best fit* for their learning, with a comparatively minimal amount of learning difficulties.

To support the learning of this group, it is recommended that interventions use the strong working memory and verbal skills of this group. A stimulating classroom environment that encourages the intrinsic motivation of Accelerated Learners is highly recommended to reduce boredom in this group. Using critical and creative-thinking strategies might be powerful tools to actively involve these students in their learning. For example, using simulations, debates, and role playing as instructional strategies creates an environment that facilitates the learning in this group. Based on their high verbal abilities, Accelerated Learners might enjoy giving presentations to demonstrate their knowledge.

Given their relative processing speed weakness, this group of students requires more time for completing assignments and taking tests. While Accelerated Learners show strengths in higher-order and creative thinking, bringing their ideas to paper might be more difficult based on fine motor difficulties, handwriting, or slower motor speed, which might be driven by perfectionistic tendencies. To address the processing speed weakness of this group, accommodations might involve untimed or oral tests, allowing students to tape record lectures rather than requiring them to take notes, as well as encouraging the use of word processors.

Cluster 6

Cluster 6 was termed Nonverbal Learning Weakness and included 13 children and adolescents who demonstrated very superior verbal abilities. This group shows a significant strength on verbal abilities (VCI = 131.08), while other areas are more evenly developed (PRI = 112.54, PSI = 108.77; WMI = 107.69). Students in Cluster 6 are likely to speak eloquently and have a well-developed vocabulary. These students are likely to be top readers, achieve excellent spelling scores, and express themselves articulately. Based on their profile, these individuals may excel during the primary years when the building blocks for learning are formed, such as learning rote facts, or reading accurately out loud. However, as these children and adolescents get older, areas of weakness are likely to exert growing influences on the academic achievement of this group, and they may increasingly experience processing difficulties that resemble or meet criteria for a nonverbal learning disability. Thus, as these students move into higher grades, where less information is *spelled out* for them, their rote memory strength, which served them well in the lower grades begins to fail them when academic demands shift to more complex applications that require them to interpret and evaluate information.

Children with nonverbal learning weakness may struggle getting the gist of things and understanding things at a conceptual level. They have difficulty organizing the visual-spatial field, adapting to new or novel situations, and accurately reading nonverbal signals or cues. As the material gets increasingly more difficult, these students may struggle with deeper, more integrative thinking. Thus, as academics become more demanding, these students may no longer be able to use their areas of strength to compensate for their weaknesses, which may be observable through a pattern of declining achievement test scores and classroom grades. However, based on their ability to use their excellent verbal abilities to compensate for their nonverbal weaknesses, these students often remain unrecognized until they reach a point in school where they can no longer function given their limitations.

Concurrent with increasing academic difficulties, students with nonverbal learning weakness may experience more anxiety and social difficulties as they get older. In addition, these individuals often struggle with social skills, which are normally grasped intuitively through observation rather than being explicitly taught. As young children, individuals with nonverbal learning weakness may often appear confused despite a high verbal intelligence because of their social ineptness brought about by misinterpretations of body language and tone of voice. These students struggle perceiving subtle cues in their environment, such as the idea of personal space, the facial expressions of others, or when others are registering pleasure/displeasure in a nonverbal mode. Instead of sensing and interpreting another individual's social cues, these students rely on their memory of past experiences, each of which is labeled verbally, to guide them in future situations.

An additional trait of children in the Nonverbal Learning Weakness subtype includes cumbersome monologues, and teachers commonly complain that these children and adolescents talk incessantly. Moreover, because of their visual-spatial weaknesses, these students have difficulty changing from one activity to another or moving from one place to another. As a result, students with nonverbal learning weakness have an increased risk of being labeled *behavior problems* or *emotionally disturbed* because of their frequent inappropriate and unexpected conduct. Also, based on the adults around them misunderstanding the ability pattern of this group, these students are commonly told that they could do better if they really tried. This frequently leads to frustration in these children and can contribute to a plummeting self-image, isolation, and withdrawal, particularly as school failures begin to multiply and intensify. Consequently, the importance of identifying and servicing this group is especially acute because overestimates of the abilities of students with nonverbal learning weakness, unrealistic demands made by parents and teachers, and mislabeling of this group can lead to ongoing emotional problems including depression, withdrawal, and anxiety.

Based on the fact that academic performance likely becomes difficult for this group as academic demands increase, recognizing the ability discrepancy of students with nonverbal learning weakness and employing interventions early in their schooling become important to maximize academic success and reduce the risk of social-emotional problems. However, it is often difficult for these individuals to receive the modifications and accommodations they require based on their above average academic achievement, especially during the early elementary years. Although these students demonstrate deficits in motor, visual-spatial, and social skills, these weaknesses frequently do not qualify this group for Special Education support services. Yet, when the verbal strengths of these students can be capitalized upon, and their unique needs are addressed, these individuals can be quite successful academically. Effective interventions for students with nonverbal learning weakness include direct verbal training in planning, organizing, studying, written expression, social cognition, and interpersonal communication.

More specific compensations and accommodations to address the weaknesses of this group include: allowing additional time to get to places and giving verbal cues to aid navigation through space; providing verbal compensatory strategies to help these students more effectively manage novel situations; avoiding power struggles and threatening; emphasizing active verbalization or subvocalization rather than mere copying of text as most effective memory approaches for this group; using graph paper to keep columns aligned in written math assignments; keeping paper and pencil tasks to a minimum because of finger dexterity and visual-spatial problems; considering occupational therapy for younger children; engaging in verbally mediated practices to improve handwriting and to increase control and fluency; using a computer word processor for written school assignments; providing additional time for written assignments; utilizing a *parts-to-whole* verbal teaching approach; making all expectations very direct and explicit rather than requiring the child to *read between the lines*; providing a predictable schedule and preparing the students in advance for changes in routine, such as assemblies, field trips, or vacation days; encouraging contact with peers to further social development; and providing cooperative learning situations.

Cluster 7

Cluster 7 was termed High General Ability and includes 13 children and adolescents with verbal and perceptual strengths (VCI = 139.85, PRI = 128.85). High General Ability students show strengths on verbal comprehension and perceptual reasoning, the areas typically considered to be indicative of giftedness. These children have very robust verbal and nonverbal intellectual skills and have a high potential to succeed in the classroom, including language based subjects and mathematics. High General Ability students have well developed verbal and reasoning skills and perform well with oral and nonverbal material. These children and adolescents are equally strong at learning facts and understanding the particulars of an idea as they are at taking varied approaches and understanding the larger context.

The high verbal comprehension index of this group indicates strong crystallized intelligence, which refers to strong acquired verbal knowledge of a culture through education and general life experiences and its effective application. This group has a strong lexical knowledge, language development, knowledge of general information, and ability to comprehend orally presented information. High General Ability students easily process verbal meanings and implications, follow verbal sequences, and formulate verbal responses. They have strong skills in organizing information sequentially, which facilitates their ability to receive, process, and communicate information. For example, when taking notes during a lecture, these students easily organize the content into major topics and subtopics and distinguish core content from peripheral material. High General Ability students have a strong ability to form and recognize concepts, perceive relationships among patterns, draw inferences, comprehend implications, solve problems, extrapolate, and reorganize or transform information, as reflected by their superior perceptual reasoning skills. These children and adolescents show a strong ability in processing, organizing, and reasoning with visually presented nonverbal material and easily solve tasks that cannot be performed automatically. While individuals in the High General Ability subtype are very bright, they show some difficulty in the areas of working memory and processing speed, which makes it difficult for these students to hold variables in mind while processing information. High General Ability students likely come across to others as being very bright and capable, and their struggles in the areas of working memory and processing speed may be perceived as a surprise. Thus, there is the risk that these students get shamed because parents and teachers do not understand their weaknesses and believe that these students simply say things to get out of trouble, when in actuality students in the High General Ability subtype are bad problem-solvers in real time. Thus, based on their areas of weakness, these students struggle processing contingencies in real time and experience the world as moving too fast for them. They struggle with accepting changing circumstances and therefore have difficulty developing adaptive responses quickly enough. High General Ability students particularly show difficulty with things that are novel and look different to them on a surface level. Thus, while these students are very bright and have an incredibly high capacity for processing information, their skills required for the process of learning are much weaker.

This group struggles to apprehend and hold information in immediate awareness. Thus, it is difficult for these students to temporarily store information and to perform a set of cognitive operations on information that requires divided attention and the management of the limited capacity of short-term memory. The high verbal comprehension, yet low working memory ability of the High General Ability group may indicate that these children and adolescents can retrieve information but have trouble encoding the information. Thus, the stores of knowledge are likely the result of repeated practice using a number of meaningful associations. High General Ability students may have difficulty filtering incoming environmental stimuli, struggling to sort trivial from important information. Thus, these students may attend to irrelevant information while ignoring the important. In addition, this group may struggle to retain or code short sequences of information long enough to stash it into a more permanent location. When meaningless data enters into working memory through a faulty filter, these students may become bewildered trying to coax the information into long-term memory. Frequently, efficient storage of new information into long-term memory requires either that material is presented repeatedly or that the child is able to closely attend to the presented material. Areas that are of particular interest to the student often facilitate sustained attention to the topic, and information is more likely to be organized in a personally meaningful way that facilitates retrieval.

On reading and writing tasks, students in the High General Ability group may do well with known topics but poorly on new ones. Additionally, due to their difficulty holding information in immediate awareness long enough to use it, children with this pattern of performance may have difficulty efficiently copying information from written material or recording information from a lecture or from the board. Finally, High General Ability students may struggle with a *bottom-up* teaching approach where the component parts of a general concept are presented separately and sequentially. This teaching approach may cause particular difficulty primarily because these individuals cannot hold the component parts in memory long enough to synthesize them into the whole concept.

Teaching to the verbal and visual reasoning strengths of the High General Ability group while bypassing, compensating for, and remediating the working memory and performance speed weaknesses of this group is recommended. Based on the working memory weakness of High General Ability students, modifications should involve changing the environment to be more engaging or giving students props to help them focus. For example, in the classroom setting, it is important to gain students' attention at the start of a lesson. Simply giving lectures or directions is commonly unsuccessful in engaging and holding students' attention. In contrast, initial activities should focus on inviting students into the lesson by creating meaningful contexts where learners can successfully connect ideas to prior understanding and form new concepts. In addition, adjusting the physical environment by providing different seating (e.g., a bean bag chair or a work station where there is little noise or distraction) can have a very beneficial impact on students' ability to focus. Other accommodations may involve letting students doodle during a lecture, holding clay or an elastic band in their hands, or chewing gum, particularly during listening activities.

Additional instructional strategies that might be useful for the High General Ability subtype include ensuring that the student is attending to the task at hand, providing succinct directions, ensuring that the child has retained sufficient information from a set of instructions to work independently, providing written directions to supplement oral directions, supplementing oral presentations and lectures by writing important information on the board, making connections between new information and prior knowledge, repeating important information often, using intonation in voice to emphasize key points, allowing multiple exposures to new material, encouraging the child to immediately record key information presented in a lecture or in reading materials, allowing extra time for copying information, breaking instructions into parts, and using a top-down approach for presenting new concepts in which the entire concept is presented first, followed by the component parts (Flanagan & Kaufman, 2004).

Cluster Validation

A comparison of subtypes by gender, ethnicity, and age indicated that individuals in Cluster 4 (mean age = 7.38 years) are referred for neuropsychological testing at a significantly younger age than students in Cluster 6 (mean age = 11.92 years). It is likely that this difference is because children in Cluster 4 begin to struggle earlier and therefore are referred for testing at an earlier age. Given that 50% of the individuals in this subtype carried a secondary diagnosis of Learning Disability, it is particularly likely that these students began showing difficulties in first and second grade when they struggled to acquire reading and writing skills. In contrast, as discussed earlier, individuals in Cluster 6 are, based on their strong verbal abilities, typically able to compensate for their weaknesses early in their academic careers. As a result, these students frequently remain unrecognized until academic demands become too large. Also, this group is often referred based on social or emotional difficulties, while their struggles with nonverbal abilities go unnoticed. Social-emotional difficulties present in this subtype may include anxiety, low self-esteem, and social skills deficits due to misinterpretation of nonverbal cues, frustration, and behavior problems.

Clinical Implications

While the presence of cluster subtypes should not form the basis for making a diagnosis of twice-exceptionality, they are clinically useful in alerting a clinician to certain diagnostic possibilities and in providing information about the pattern of strengths and weaknesses that characterize twice-exceptional children and adolescents. The lack of a clear description of twice-exceptional students has precluded the correct identification of several of these children and adolescents. A comprehensive assessment battery is needed to identify and plan interventions for this group. Ideally, early identification and appropriate interventions are employed to prevent social and behavioral problems in these students.

Twice-exceptional children and adolescents present a paradoxical picture of exceptional strengths coexisting with specific deficits. These students may use their gifts and talents to compensate for their deficits and overcome their academic difficulties with support, understanding, and instructional interventions and accommodations. However, because these students are frequently able to utilize their strengths to compensate for their weaker areas, deficits commonly remain unrecognized, misunderstood, and underserved. Consequently, diagnosticians, including psychologists, audiologists, optometrists, and occupational therapists need to be aware of the compensatory behaviors this group may employ and inspect how their weaker areas compare to their stronger areas. Likewise, it is important to recognize that among twice-exceptional children with high abilities in certain areas, scores in the average range on the WISC-IV may be sufficient to indicate a deficit. While an average score does not constitute a deficit when compared to the population in general, it can indicate a significant personal weakness compared to the student's abilities in other areas. For example, a factor index score in the lower end of the Average Range (i.e., 85-90) is a significant relative weakness for a student whose other standard scores are in the High Average or Superior Range (i.e., 125-140). In addition, the observed factor scatter may be so large that it is not commonly found in the normal population, despite the lowest score still being in the average range. Therefore, the child's identified weakness should play an essential role in developing educational interventions and accommodations. Otherwise, there is a risk that the correctable deficits of twice-exceptional children and adolescents who score within the average range on their assessments are not recognized.

To improve services for twice-exceptional children and adolescents, it is important to shift away from using rigid definitions and cutoff scores to specify qualification for special programming and services. Instead, broader definitions of giftedness are needed to ensure that twice-exceptional children and adolescents are recognized and receive the services they need. Twice-exceptional students would benefit from individualized programs focusing on building on their talents, while at the same time remediating their areas of weakness. In addition, due to their variable cognitive profiles, it is important that twice-exceptional children and adolescents receive support for their unique social and emotional needs.

Twice-exceptional children and adolescents, with their paradoxical combination of gifts and weaknesses, are considered vulnerable to negative emotional and social outcomes such as poor self-concept, poor self-efficacy, hypersensitivity, emotional lability, and heightened frustration, anxiety, and self-criticism (Dole, 2000). Twice-exceptional students are more likely to be aware of their weaknesses and varied abilities, which can create frustration, upset, low self-esteem, and depression. Emotional factors may further impact the relationships of twice-exceptional students with family members and peers. For example, twice-exceptional children and adolescents may struggle to fit in with their peers and experience loneliness or rejection. As a result, many twice-exceptional students benefit from access to various counseling services including individual, group, or family counseling. It is important that professionals working with twice-exceptional children and adolescents understand their increased risk for having social-emotional problems.

Emotionally, due to the academic difficulties with which many twice-exceptional students struggle, these children and adolescents commonly lose confidence in their ability to succeed. Particularly, twice-exceptional students with a big spread within their cognitive abilities may be sensitive to failure and be troubled by the vast discrepancy between what they can and cannot do (Olenchak, 1994). This misconception of their abilities can lead to feelings of frustration and confusion over their varying abilities. In addition, perfectionism, which is frequently present among twice-exceptional students, can cause them to feel that none of their efforts are adequate. These experiences can lead to depression, feelings of failure, inadequacy, worthlessness, and anger, as well as acting-out behaviors to disguise feelings of low self-esteem and self-efficacy (Nielsen, 2002).

Given the increased risk for emotional problems, twice-exceptional students may need professional help to reconcile their frustrations and perceived failures. For example, many twice-exceptional children and adolescents might benefit from learning specific coping skills to help them handle their frustrations caused by high expectations for themselves. Also, twice-exceptional students may benefit from expressing their feelings, concerns, and frustrations creatively, such as through art, music, or journal writing. Sharing ability test results with these individuals and highlighting their particular strengths, combined with reassurance, may foster a more appropriate sense of self-evaluation in this population. In addition, these students will benefit if their differences in ability are responded to with supportive parenting and teaching. Families and schools that cherish the individual differences of twice-exceptional students will allow these children and adolescents to learn to value their uniqueness.

The emotional problems of low self-concept, frustration, anger, and resentment twice-exceptional students tend to experience may not only influence the behavior of these students, but can also impact relations with peers and family members. This is particularly true for students in Cluster 1, Verbal Learners, who demonstrate the largest factor scatter among all twice-exceptional subtypes. The significant processing speed weakness of Verbal Learners, compared to their strong verbal skills can lead to frustration and low self-esteem in this group of students. Also, twice-exceptional children and adolescents may commonly suffer from a lack of social skills, which may cause them to become loners or troublemakers (Baum, Cooper, Neu, & Owen 1997). Their difficulty with social skills may stem from difficulties perceiving social cues that inform behavior, or lack of confidence in their own abilities causing them to act out to hide their weaknesses (Olenchak, 1994). Children in Cluster 6, Nonverbal Learning Weakness, are at particular risk for social skills deficits. Despite their high verbal intelligence, students in this group have difficulty reading body language and grasping social cues. As a result, this group of students may act socially awkward or engage in socially inappropriate behaviors. The social skills deficits of these children and adolescents can further contribute to low self-image, isolation, withdrawal, or anxiety. To address social difficulties, it is recommended that twice-exceptional students are given the opportunity to interact with peers who share similar strengths and interests. In educational settings, it might be particularly helpful to allow students to work together on a project to foster teamwork and sharing. Activities allowing teamwork provide the opportunity for students to recognize that each team member has something valuable to contribute to the team's success, which can foster not only social skills, but also self-esteem (Gentry & Neu, 1998). In addition, twice-exceptional students may benefit from support in establishing and maintaining social relationships. For example, social skills training aiding twice-exceptional students in interacting more appropriately with their peers might be beneficial to their overall social-emotional functioning.

Educational Implications

It is hoped that the seven twice-exceptional subtypes identified in the present study will facilitate educational decisions being rendered for this population. The appropriate identification of strengths and weaknesses allows twice-exceptional children and adolescents to benefit from educational programs that are flexible and individualized to their specific needs. More specifically, education programs should foster the talents of this group, provide developmental instruction in areas of average growth, and offer remedial and adaptive teaching in areas of deficits. In addition, as is true for all children with special needs, including the gifted and twice-exceptional populations, early intervention provides the best opportunity for optimal development (Silverman, 1998). Thus, as early as during the preschool and primary years, twice-exceptional students would benefit from a curriculum that nurtures their strengths, while accommodating for their areas of weakness. A comprehensive program should provide a learning environment valuing individual talents, educational support including compensatory strategies for areas of weakness, and school based counseling services to address the mix of talents and weaknesses this group experiences (NAGC, 1998).

Because of concerns with students' disabilities, such as ADHD or Learning Disorder, well-intentioned teachers commonly ignore the gifts of twice-exceptional children and adolescents. Teachers frequently believe that weaknesses must be addressed and remediated before any focus can be directed toward the strengths of these students. However, research suggests that learning strategies employed for twice-exceptional students should accommodate both areas of strengths and weaknesses simultaneously to creating an appropriate balance of attention between the two abilities (Baum et al., 1991, 2001). A focus on a student's weaknesses without a similar focus on the development of strengths can result in poor self-esteem, lack of motivation, depression, and stress (Gardynik & McDonald, 2005). Teaching to students' abilities rather than weaknesses can increase these students' self-concept and motivation, while concurrently improving basic skills (Baum, Emerick, Herman, & Dixon, 1989). Providing these students with strategies to use their strengths to compensate for areas of weaknesses is another important factor that can help these students succeed. Strengths and talents should be nurtured, while students learn to effectively compensate for their weaker areas (Baum et al., 1991). Additionally, it is important for twice-exceptional students to attend programs in nurturing and supportive environments that allow them to feel valued and provide respect for the individual differences of this population.

A curriculum best suited for this population should be challenging enough to engage twice-exceptional students in their learning, while providing accommodations for areas of weakness to achieve a balance between the diverse learning needs of this group (Baum et al., 2001). It is recommended that twice-exceptional students receive access to enriched curricula focusing on their areas of strength for at least a portion of each school day or week. Research recommends that twice-exceptional students are viewed as gifted first, and their areas of strengths are fostered in the classroom setting. Focusing on the strengths of these students, rather than emphasizing areas of weakness, ensures that academic skill acquisition, self-esteem, and critical and creative thinking abilities of these students are addressed appropriately (Nielsen, 2002). In addition, through self-understanding of their strengths and weaknesses, twice-exceptional students can develop resilience and the ability to adapt and compensate for weaker areas.

To address the disparate strengths and weaknesses of twice-exceptional children and adolescents, these students will likely need a unique curriculum of enrichment, acceleration, and remediation to address their varied abilities. Enrichment opportunities may include participation in a school's pull-out gifted program, the assignment of special in-depth projects, or guided work on areas of interest to the student. Accelerative strategies may involve grade skipping, specific-subject acceleration, self-paced instruction in particular curricular areas, or mentoring. Support and remediation options may include accommodations (additional time on tasks) or interventions through special education (Volker et al., 2006). Also, school teams may want to create individualized educational programs (IEPs) for twice-exceptional students that fit the unique pattern of strengths and weaknesses of these children and adolescents.

Specific strategies to enhance areas of gifts and talents of twice-exceptional students include designing curricula that recognize and enhance different learning styles, emphasizing critical and creative thinking; allowing students to self-select projects; allowing students opportunities to conduct in-depth exploration within interest areas; teaching students to recognize, access, and utilize their talents to help them bypass or compensate for their areas of weakness; encouraging students to recognize, accept, and appreciate their gifts and talents; and modifying assignments so that gifts and talents can be demonstrated.

To address areas of weaknesses of twice-exceptional children and adolescents, the following accommodations are recommended: allowing students to take tests in a quiet setting, allowing more time to complete tests, using graphic organizers, teaching specific organizational strategies (e.g., webbing, storyboarding, appointment books), teaching study and test-taking strategies, allowing more time to complete reading and paper-and-pencil assignments, dividing assignments so students do not get overwhelmed, avoiding excessive use of worksheets, accompanying oral directions with written directions to which students can later refer, presenting reading assignments on cassette tapes, and incorporating multisensory instruction (e.g., video, tape recordings, music, hands-on experiences).

In addition, several behavior management strategies have been recommended including: providing assignment-management plans to assist students in organizing long-term assignments; avoiding placing students under pressure of competition; arranging a regular time to talk privately with students regarding their behavior; providing clear information about what behavior is acceptable and consistently reinforcing that behavior;

ignoring inappropriate behavior that is not drastically outside classroom limits; providing a quiet, neutral area in the room where students can go to *cool off;* allowing students to participate in decisions; and providing students with acceptable ways to show their creativity without disrupting the classroom (Nielsen, 2002). Lastly, to address the social and emotional needs of twice-exceptional learners, educators should focus on creating emotionally safe, consistent, and predictable environments; providing instruction in social skill development; assisting students in the exploration of strategies for coping with change; enhancing and building on students' leadership skills; and focusing on developing collaboration skills.

Limitations

There are a number of possible limitations in this investigation that should be considered when interpreting the results. First of all, participants for the present study included individuals referred for comprehensive neuropsychological testing, which may have biased the sample toward relatively more severe symptomatology. Consequently, the degree to which the findings will generalize to samples of non-referred twice-exceptional children and adolescents is unknown. Also, the sample sizes of some of the seven clusters were relatively low; and the majority of children and adolescents in the present sample were male (83.3%) and White (88.9%). Consequently, findings from the present study may not generalize to more diverse samples of twice-exceptional students.

A further limitation of the present study is that it does not establish the diagnostic utility of the extracted profiles. Diagnostic utility needs to be established through demonstrating that the subtypes prescribe useful interventions or predict future outcomes. It is suggested that future research attempt to replicate the seven twice-exceptional subtypes extracted in the current study and identify potentially helpful interventions for the different subtypes.

While ability testing remains the most unbiased method available for identifying twice-exceptional students, it is important to recognize that intelligence tests should only be part of a comprehensive assessment of children and adolescents. The emphasis on intelligence tests in the present study does in no way imply that intelligence tests scores should be the sole factor used to identify twice-exceptional children nor the primary factor used in decision-making about eligibility for services or programs. Given the heterogeneity of the cognitive ability of twice-exceptional students identified in this study, it is recommended that a complete assessment is utilized to identify and plan interventions for twice-exceptional children and adolescents. Identification of twice-exceptional students, as well as decision-making about eligibility for services should in addition to ability testing and other test data include behavioral observation, interviews, case histories, and subjective evaluation of a child's abstract thought processes, intensity, complexity, sensitivity, and awareness.

Future Research

Future research should attempt to validate the seven twice-exceptional subtypes extracted in the present study through replication in an independent sample. Studies should focus on including a diverse sample in terms of gender, ethnicity, and geographic location. Replication of the cluster solution identified in the current study will lend support toward the reliability and validity of the seven twice-exceptional profiles. Questions of treatment responsiveness and more complete neuropsychological functioning profiles also merit consideration.

An additional area for future research is the exploration of overlap between identified subtypes with specific diagnostic groups such as ADHD, LD, or Asperger's Disorder. Findings of the present suggest that certain diagnoses (e.g., ADHD) appear to be more common among certain cluster subtypes. It is recommended that future research investigate more closely the presentation and overlap of diagnoses. Future research might examine the diagnostic utility of the subtypes identified in this study by investigating whether subtypes prescribe useful interventions or predict future outcomes.

Based on the strength and weakness patterns identified for the seven twice-exceptional subtypes, it is recommended that future research more closely examine the effectiveness of interventions and accommodations suggested for the different subtypes. Research examining academic as well as social-emotional functioning of students receiving support for their areas of weakness, while also challenging areas of strengths by utilizing some of the recommendations provided in this study is highly recommended.

Lastly, research examining the performance of twice-exceptional subtypes identified in this study on other measures would be beneficial. Performance on achievement tests or neuropsychological tests in the areas of memory, attention, executive functioning, or language would further the knowledge of this underserved group of students. More complete neuropsychological functioning profiles would allow a greater understanding of the specific strength and weakness patterns present in this population and to further improve identification and provision of services to this group.

REFERENCES

Ackerman, C. M., & Paulus, L. E. (1997). Identifying gifted adolescents using personality characteristics: Dabrowski's overexcitabilities. *Roeper Review, 19*(4), 229-237.

Aldenderfer, M. S., & Blashfield, R. K. (1984). *Cluster analysis.* Newbury Park, CA: Sage Publications.

American Psychiatric Association. (2000). *Diagnostic and statistical manual of mental disorders* (4th ed., text revision). Washington, DC: Author.

Anastasi, A. (1982). *Psychological testing.* New York, NY: Macmillan.

Bannatyne, A. (1971). *Language, reading, and learning disabilities.* Springfield, IL: Thomas.

Bannatyne, A. (1974). Diagnosis: A note on recategorizing of the WISC-R scaled scores. *Journal of Learning Disabilities, 7,* 272-274.

Barkley, R. A. (1994). *ADHD in the classroom: Strategies for teachers.* New York, NY: Guilford Press.

Barton, J. M., & Starnes, W. T. (1988). Identifying distinguishing characteristics of gifted and talented/learning disabled students. *Roeper Review, 12*(1), 23-29.

Barton, J. M., & Starnes, W. T. (1989). Identifying distinguishing characteristics of gifted and talented/learning disabled students. *Roeper Review, 12*(1), 23-29.

Baum, S. (1990). *Gifted but learning disabled: A puzzling paradox.* (ERIC EC Digest #E479). Arlington, VA: The ERIC Clearinghouse on Disabilities and Gifted Education.

Baum, S. (1994). Meeting the needs of gifted/learning disabled students. *The Journal of Secondary Gifted Education, 5*(3), 6-16.

Baum, S. M., Cooper, C. R., & Neu, T. W. (2001). Dual differentiation: An approach for meeting the curricular needs of gifted students with learning disabilities. *Psychology in the Schools, 38*, 477-490.

Baum, S., Cooper, C., Neu, T., & Owen, S. (1997). *Evaluation of Project High Hopes. (Project R206A30159-95).* Washington, DC: U.S. Department of Education (OERI).

Baum, S., Emerick, L. J., Herman, G. N., & Dixon, J. (1989). Identification, programs, and enrichment strategies for gifted learning disabled youth. *Roeper Review, 12*(1), 48-53.

Baum, S. M., & Olenchak, F. R. (2002). The alphabet children: GT, ADD/ADHD, and more. *Exceptionality, 10*(2), 77-91.

Baum, S. M., & Owen, S. V. (2004). *To be gifted and learning disabled: Strategies for helping bright students with LD, ADHD, and more.* Mansfield Center, CT: Creative Learning Press.

Baum, S., Owen, S. V., & Dixon, J. (1991). *To be gifted and learning disabled: From definitions to practical intervention strategies.* Mansfield Center, CT: Creative Learning Press.

Blakely, T. A., Crinella, F. M., Fisher, T. D., Champaigne, L., & Beck, F. W. (1994). Neuropsychological correlates of learning disabilities: Subtype identification by the Tryon clustering method. *Journal of Developmental and Physical Diabilities, 6*(1), 1-22.

Brody, L. E., & Mills, C. J. (1997). Gifted children with learning disabilities: A review of the issues. *Journal of Learning Disabilities, 30*(3), 282-296.

Brown, S. E., & Yakimowski, M. E. (1987). Intelligence scores of gifted students on the WISC-R. *Gifted Child Quarterly, 31*, 130-134.

Calhoun, S. L., & Mayes, S. D. (2005). Processing speed in children with clinical disorders. *Psychology in the Schools, 42*(4), 333-343.

Cohen, S. S., & Vaughn, S. (1994). Gifted students with learning disabilities: What does the research say? *Learning Disabilities: A Multidisciplinary Journal, 5*, 87-94.

Cronbach, L. J. (1984). *Essentials of psychological testing.* New York, NY: Harper & Row.

Cronbach, L. J., & Gleser, G. C. (1953). Assessing similarity between profiles. *Psychological Bulletin, 50 (6),* 456-473.

Dabrowski, K. (1964). *Positive disintegration.* Boston, MA: Little, Brown.

Dabrowski, K. (1967). *Personality shaping through positive disintegration.* Boston, MA: Little, Brown.

Davis (Eds.), *Handbook of gifted education* (3rd ed., pp. 533-543). Boston, MA: Allyn & Bacon.

Dole, S. (2000). The implications of the risk and resilience literature for gifted students with learning disabilities. *Roeper Review, 23*(2), 91-96.

Donders, J. (1996). Cluster subtypes in the WISC-III standardization sample: Analysis of factor index scores. *Psychological Assessment, 8*(3), 312-318.

Epstein, M. H. (1999). The development and validation of a scale to assess the emotional and behavioral strengths of children and adolescents. *Remedial and Special Education, 20*, 258-262.

Fishkin, A. S., Kampsnider, J. J., & Pack, L. (1996). Exploring the WISC-III as a measure of giftedness. *Roeper Review, 18*(3), 226-231.

Flanagan, D. P., & Harrison, P. L. (2005). *Contemporary intellectual assessment: Theories, tests, and issues.* New York, NY: Guilford Press.

Flanagan, D. P., & Kaufman, A. S. (2004). *Essentials of WISC-IV assessment.* Hoboken, NJ: John Wiley & Sons.

Fox, L. H. (1983). Gifted students with reading problems. In L. H. Fox, L. Brody, & D. Tobin (Eds.), *Learning-disabled/gifted children: Identification and programming* (pp. 117-139). Austin, TX: PRO-ED.

Fox, J. J., Gunter, P., Davis, C. A., & Brall, S. (2000). Observational methods in functional behavioral assessment: Practical techniques for practitioners. *Preventing School Failure, 44*, 152-157.

Gallagher, P. A. (1997). Promoting dignity: Taking the destructive D's out of behavior disorders. *Focus on Exceptional Children, 29*, 1-19.

Gardner, H. (1983). *Frames of mind: The theory of multiple intelligences.* New York, NY: Basic Books.

Gardner, H. (1999). *Intelligences reframed: Multiple intelligences.* New York, NY: Basic Books.

Gardynik, U. M., & McDonald, L. (2005). Implications of risk and resilience in the life of the individual who is gifted/learning disabled. *Roeper Review, 27*(4), 206-214.

Gentry, M., & Neu, T. (1998). Project High Hopes summer institute: Curriculum for developing talent in students with special needs. *Roeper Review 20*(4), 291-295.

Glutting, J. J., Konold, T. R., McDermott, P. A., Kush, J. C., & Watkins, M. M. (1999). Structure and diagnostic benefits of a normative subtest taxonomy developed from the WISC-III standardization sample. *Journal of School Psychology, 37*, 29-48.

Glutting, J. J., & McDermott, P. A. (1990). Patterns and prevalence of core profile types in the WPPSI standardization sample. *School Psychology Review, 19*, 471-491.

Glutting, J. J., & McDermott, P. A., Prifitera, A., & McGrath, E. A. (1994). Core profile types for the WISC-III and WIAT: Their development and application in identifying multivariate IQ-achievement discrepancies. *School Psychology Review, 23*, 610-639.

Glutting, J. J., McDermott, P. A., Watkins, M. M., Kush, J. C., & Konold, T. R. (1997). The base rate problem and its consequences for interpreting children's ability profiles. *School Psychology Review, 26*, 176-188.

Hale, J. B., Fiorello, C. F., Kavanagh, J. A., Hoeppner, J. B., & Gaither, R. A. (2001). WISC-III predictors of academic achievement for children with learning disabilities: Are global and factor scores comparable? *School Psychology Quarterly, 16*, 31-55.

Hollingworth, L. S. (1928). *The psychology of the adolescent.* New York, NY: D. Appleton and Company.

Hollingworth, H. L. (1943). *Leta Stetter Hollingworth*. Lincoln, NE: University of Nebraska Press.

Huberty, C. J., DiStefano, C., & Kamphaus, R. W. (1997). Behavioral clustering of school children. *Multivariate Behavioral Research, 32*(2), 105-134.

Individuals with Disabilities Education Improvement Act of 2004 (IDEA). (2004). Retrieved from http://frwebgate.access.gpo.gov/cgi-bin/getdoc.cgi

Kamphaus, R. W., Petoskey, M. D., & Walters Morgan, A. (1997). A history of intelligence test interpretation. In D. F. Flanagan, J. L. Genshaft, & P. L. Harrison (Eds.), *Contemporary intellectual assessment: Theories, tests, and issues* (pp. 32-48). New York, NY: Guilford Press.

Kaufman, A. S. (1975). Factor analysis of the WISC-R at 11 age levels between 6½ and 16½. *Journal of Consulting and Clinical Psychology, 43*, 135-147.

Kaufman, A. S. (1976). A new approach to the interpretation of test scatter on the WISC-R. *Journal of Learning Disabilities, 9*, 160-168.

Kaufman, A. S. (1979). WISC-R research: Implications for interpretation. *School Psychology Digest, 15*, 176-179.

Kaufman, A. S. (1992). Evaluation of the WISC-III and WPPSI-R for gifted children. *Roeper Review, 14*, 154-158.

Kaufman, A. S. (1994). *Intelligent testing with the WISC-III*. New York, NY: John Wiley & Sons.

Konold, T. R., Glutting, J. J., McDermott, P. A., Kush, J. C., & Watkins, M. M. (1999). Structure and diagnostic benefits of a normative subtest taxonomy developed from the WISC-III standardization sample. *Journal of School Psychology, 37,* 29-48.

Kramer, J. H. (1993). Interpretation of individual subtest scores on the WISC-III. *Psychological Assessment, 5,* 193-196.

Lovett, B. J., & Lewandowski, L. J. (2006). Gifted students with learning disabilities: Who are they? *Journal of learning disabilities, 39,* 515-527.

Marland, S. P. (1972). *Education of the gifted and talented* (Report to the Subcommittee on Education, Committee on Labor and Public Welfare, U.S. Senate). Washington, DC: U.S. Government Printing Office.

Mayes, S. D., & Calhoun, S. L. (2003). Analysis of WISC-III, Stanford Binet IV, and academic achievement test scores in children with autism. *Journal of Autism and Developmental Disorders, 33,* 329-341.

Mayes, S. D., Calhoun, S. L., & Crowell, E. W. (1998). WISC-III profiles for children with and without learning disabilities. *Psychology in the Schools, 35,* 309-316.

McCoach, D. B., Kehle, T. J., Bray, M. A., & Siegle, D. (2001). Best practices in the identification of gifted students with learning disabilities. *Psychology in the Schools, 38,* 403-411.

McDermott, P. A., Glutting, J. J., Jones, J. N., & Noonan, J. V. (1989). Typology and prevailing composition of core profiles in the WAIS-R standardization sample. *Psychological Assessment, 1,* 292-299.

Mealer, C., Morgan, S., & Luscomb, R. (1996). Cognitive functioning of ADHD and non-ADHD boys on the WISC-III and WRAML: An analysis within a memory model. *Journal of Attention Disorders, 1,* 133-147.

Miller, N. B., & Silverman, L. K. (1987). Levels of personality development. *Roeper Review, 9*(4), 221-225.

Moon, S. M. (2002). Counseling needs and strategies. In M. Neihart, S. Reis, N. M. Robinson, & S. M. Moon (Eds.), *The social and emotional development of gifted children: What do we know?* (pp. 213-222). Waco, TX: Prufrock Press, Inc.

Mooney, J., & Cole, D. (2000). *Learning outside the lines: Two ivy league students with learning disabilities and ADHD give you the tools for academic success and education revolution.* New York, NY: Fireside.

Morelock, M. J. (1992). Giftedness: The view from within. *Understanding our gifted, 4*(3), 1, 11-15.

Morrison, D. F. (1976). *Multivariate statistical methods.* New York, NY: McGraw-Hill.

Morrison, W. F. (2001). Emotional/behavioral disabilities and gifted and talented behaviors: Paradoxical or semantic differences in characteristics? *Psychology in the schools, 38,* 425-431.

National Association for Gifted Children (NAGC). (1998). *Students with concomitant gifts and learning disabilities.* Washington, DC: Author.

Neihart, M. (1999). The impact of giftedness on psychological well-being: What does the empirical literature say? *Roeper Review, 22*(1), 10-17.

Nielsen, M. E. (2002). Gifted students with learning disabilities: Recommendations for identification and programming. *Exceptionality, 10,* 93-111.

Norusis, M. J. (1995). *SPSS professional statistics 7.1.* Chicago, IL: SPSS, Inc.

Nyden, A., Billstedt, E., Hjelmquist, E., & Gillberg, C. (2001). Neurocognitive stability in Asperger syndrome, ADHD, and reading and writing disorder: A pilot study. *Developmental Medicine and Child Neurology, 43,* 165-171.

Olenchak, F. R. (1994). Talent development: Accommodating the social and emotional needs of secondary gifted learning disabled students. *The Journal of Secondary Gifted Education, 5,* 40-52.

Osborne, J. K., & Byrnes, D. A. (1990). Identifying gifted and talented students in an alternative learning center. *Gifted Child Quarterly, 34*(4), 143, 146.

Ozonoff, S. (1998). Treatment of executive dysfunction. In E. Schopler, G. B. Mesibov, & L. Kunce (Eds.), *Asperger syndrome or high-functioning autism* (pp. 263-289). New York, NY: Plenum Press.

Patchett, R. F., & Stansfield, M. (1992). Subtest scatter on the WISC-R with children of superior intelligence. *Psychology in the Schools, 29,* 5-10.

Piirto, J. (2004). *Understanding creativity.* Scottsdale, AZ: Great Potential Press.

Prifitera, A., & Saklofske, D. H. (1998). *WISC-III clinical use and interpretation.* San Diego, CA: Academic Press.

Rapaport, D., Gill, M. M., & Schafer, R. (1946). *Diagnostic psychological testing.* Chicago, IL: Year Book.

Reid, B. (1995). *Square pegs in round holes-these kids don't fit: Bright students with behavior problems.* Presentation at the National Association for Gifted Children, Tampa, FL.

Reis, S. M., & McCoach, D. B. (2002). Underachievement in gifted and talented students with special needs. *Exceptionality, 10*(2), 113-125.

Renzulli, J. S. (1986). The three-ring conception of giftedness: A developmental model for productive creativity. In R. J. Sternberg & J. E. Davidson (Eds.), *Conceptions of giftedness* (pp. 53-92). New York, NY: Cambridge University Press.

Rizza, M. G., & Morrison, W. F. (2003). Uncovering stereotypes and identifying characteristics of gifted students and students with emotional/behavioral disabilities. *Roeper Review, 25*(2), 73-77.

Robinson, B. R., & Harrison, P. L. (2005). WISC-III core profiles for students referred or found eligible for special education and gifted programs. *School Psychology Quarterly, 20*(1), 51-65.

Sattler, J. M. (1988). *Assessment of children* (3rd ed.). San Diego, CA: Author.

Sattler, J. M. (1992). *Assessment of children* (3rd ed., rev.). San Diego, CA; Author.

Sattler, J. M. (2001). *Assessment of children. Cognitive applications* (4th ed.). San Diego, CA: Author.

Sattler, J. M. (2002). *Assessment of children. Behavioral and clinical implications* (4th ed.). San Diego, CA: Author.

Schiff, M. M., Kaufman, A. S., & Kaufman, N. L. (1981). Scatter analysis of WISC-R profiles for learning disabled children with superior intelligence. *Journal of Learning Disabilities, 14,* 400-404.

Seeley, K. R. (1998). Underachieving and talented learners with disabilities. In J. Van Tassel-Baska (Ed.), *Excellence in educating gifted and talented learners* (pp. 83-93). Denver, CO: Love Publishing.

Silver, S. J., & Clampit, M. K. (1990). WISC-R profiles of high ability children: Interpretation of verbal-performance discrepancies. *Gifted Children Quarterly, 34,* 76-79.

Silverman, L. K. (1989). The visual-spatial learner. *Preventing School Failure, 34*(1), 15-20.

Silverman, L. K. (1993). *Counseling the gifted and talented.* Denver, CO: Love.

Silverman, L. K. (1997). The construct of asynchronous development. *Peabody Journal of Education, 72*(3-4), 36-58.

Silverman, L. K. (1998). Through the lens of giftedness. *Roeper Review, 20*(3), 204-210.

Silverman, L. K. (2003). Gifted children with learning disabilities. In N. A. Colangelo & G. A.

Snow, J. H., Cohen, M., & Holliman, W. B. (1985). Learning disability subgroups using cluster analysis of the WISC-R. *Journal of Psychoeducational Assessment, 4,* 391-397.

Starnes, W., Ginevan, J., Stokes, L., & Barton, J. (1988). *A study in the identification, differential diagnosis, and remediation of underachieving highly able students.* Paper presented at the annual meeting of the Council for Exceptional Children, Washington, DC.

Sternberg, R. J. (1985). *Beyond I.Q.: A triarchic theory of human intelligence.* Cambridge, MA: Cambridge University Press.

Stormont, M., Stebbins, M. S., & Holliday, G. (2001). Characteristics and educational support needs of underrepresented gifted adolescents. *Psychology in the Schools, 38,* 413-423.

Tannenbaum, A. J. (1991). The social psychology of giftedness. In N. Colangelo & G. A. Davis (Eds.), *Handbook of gifted education* (pp. 27-44). Toronto, Canada: Allyn & Bacon.

Terman, L. M. (1925). *Genetic studies of genius: The mental and physical traits of a thousand gifted children.* Stanford, CA: Stanford University Press.

The Psychological Corporation. (1999). *Wechsler Abbreviated Scale of Intelligence.* San Antonio, TX: Author.

The Psychological Corporation. (2002). *Wechsler Individual Achievement Test-Second Edition (WIAT-II).* San Antonio, TX: Author.

Thompson, L. (1971). Language disabilities in men of eminence. *Journal of Learning Disabilities, 4,* 34-45.

U.S. Office of Education. (1977). Assistance to states for education for handicapped children: Procedures for evaluating specific learning disabilities. *Federal Register, 42,* 62082-62085.

Vaughn, S. (1989). Gifted learning disabilities: Is it such a bright idea? *Learning Disabilities Focus, 4,* 123-128.

Voeller, K. K. (1994). Clinical neurologic aspects of the right-hemispheric deficit syndrome. *Journal of Child Neurology, 10,* 516-522.

Volker, M. A., Lopata, C., & Cook-Cottone, C. (2006). Assessment of children with intellectual giftedness and reading disabilities. *Psychology in the Schools, 43,* 855-869.

Waldron, K. A., & Saphire, D. G. (1990). An analysis of WISC-R factors for gifted students with learning disabilities. *Journal of Learning Disabilities, 23,* 491-498.

Ward, J. H., Jr. (1963). Hierarchical grouping to optimize an objective function. *American Statistical Association Journal, 58,* 236-244.

Ward, T. J., Ward, S. B., Glutting, J. J., & Hatt, C. V. (1999). Exceptional LD profile types for the WISC-III and WIAT. *School Psychology Review, 28,* 629-643.

Webb, J. T., Amend, E. R., Webb, N. E., Goerss, J., Beljan, P., & Olenchak, F. R. (2005). *Misdiagnosis and dual diagnoses of gifted children and adults: ADHD, Bipolar, OCD, Asperger's, depression, and other disorders.* Scottsdale, AZ: Great Potential Press.

Webb, N., & Dietrich, A. (2005). Gifted and learning disabled: A neuropsychologist's perspective. *Gifted Education Communicator, 36,* 3-4.

Wechsler, D. (1949). *Wechsler Intelligence Scale for Children.* New York, NY: Psychological Corporation.

Wechsler, D. (1974). *Manual for the Wechsler Intelligence Scale for Children-Revised.* San Antonio, TX: Psychological Corporation.

Wechsler, D. (1991). *Wechsler Intelligence Scale for Children- Third edition.* San Antonio, TX: Psychological Corporation.

Wechsler, D. (1997). *The Wechsler Adult Intelligence Scale-III: Administration and scoring manual.* San Antonio, TX: Psychological Corporation.

Wechsler, D. (2002). *Wechsler Preschool and Primary Scales of Intelligence- Third Edition (WPPSI-III): Administration and scoring manual.* San Antonio, TX: Psychological Corporation.

Wechsler, D. (2003). *WISC-IV technical and interpretive manual.* San Antonio, TX: Psychological Corporation.

Wilkinson, S. C. (1993). WISC-R profiles of children with superior intellectual ability. *Gifted Child Quarterly, 37,* 84-91.

APPENDIX A

MANUSCRIPT

The Cognitive Profiles of

Twice-Exceptional Children and Adolescents

Laura McDonald, M.A.

Beth Houskamp, Ph.D.

Sheryn Scott, Ph.D.

Robert Welsh, Ph.D.

Azusa Pacific University

Abstract

Twice-exceptionality can be defined as the co-occurrence of intellectual giftedness and disability, including academic, social-emotional, and behavioral problems. There is a lack of empirical research examining the area of twice-exceptionality; and, as a result, there is insufficient support for the current definitions, identification criteria, and interventions employed for twice-exceptional individuals. The heterogeneity of this population indicates the importance of exploring the cognitive patterns present among twice-exceptional individuals to facilitate the identification as well as the treatment of this population. The present study examined the Wechsler Intelligence Scale, Fourth Edition (WISC-IV; Wechsler, 2003) profiles of 95 twice-exceptional children and adolescents to facilitate the discovery of subtype patterns present among this group. A two-stage cluster analysis revealed 7 twice-exceptional subtypes that were differentiated primarily by level of performance on the 4 factor scores. The identified twice-exceptional subtypes provide information about characteristic strengths and weaknesses that not only facilitate the identification of twice-exceptional students, but also carry implications for educational intervention.

The Cognitive Profiles of
Twice-exceptional Children and Adolescents

Children and adolescents who exhibit intellectual giftedness in conjunction with learning, social-emotional, or behavioral disabilities are referred to as twice-exceptional. These individuals demonstrate characteristics of two exceptionalities: intellectual gifts and difficulties such as learning and attention deficits, depression, anxiety, anger, or acting out behaviors (National Association for Gifted Children [NAGC], 1998). However, gifts and deficits are typically viewed as lying at opposite ends of a spectrum; and the concept of a gifted individual with a disability is often viewed as an oxymoron (Seeley, 1998). As a result, there is a lack of knowledge regarding the characteristics of twice-exceptional individuals; and research investigating this area is needed to aid in understanding this population and to provide clearer identification criteria and suitable intervention strategies for this understudied group.

While the use of intelligence tests has been viewed as the gold standard for the identification of giftedness, a number of barriers impede the identification of twice-exceptional children and adolescents. For example, the learning, social-emotional, and behavior difficulties present in twice-exceptional individuals depress their performance on intelligence tests. Consequently, the typical Full Scale IQ cutoff score of 130 used for the identification of giftedness is not sensitive enough to identify twice-exceptional students; and it is recommended that cutoff scores are adjusted downward (Nielsen,

2002). Research investigating the identification of gifted students with learning disabilities suggests the use of scatter and profile analysis in the identification of twice-exceptional individuals (Brody & Mills, 1997; Nielsen, 2002; Silverman, 2003). More specifically, Nielsen suggested that subtest scatter of at least seven scaled-score points between highest and lowest subtest scores on the Wechsler Intelligence test and low Coding and Digit Span scores is indicative of twice-exceptionality and should be investigated further.

Research has examined the WISC factor and subtest score scatter of gifted children and gifted children with learning disabilities. No analysis has examined the cognitive ability of gifted students with behavioral or social-emotional difficulties. Research examining the discrepancy between verbal and performance IQ scores of gifted students has found large discrepancies with higher scores on the Verbal Scale (Patchett & Stansfield, 1992; Prifitera & Saklofske, 1998; Silver & Clampit, 1990). In contrast, studies investigating verbal-performance discrepancies among gifted students with learning disabilities have not found a discrepancy specific to this group but, instead, discovered mixed results (Barton & Starnes, 1989; Fox, 1983; Schiff, Kaufman, & Kaufman, 1981). In addition, verbal and performance scores are frequently viewed as obscuring an individual's cognitive ability because they lump together several areas of functioning that may then lead to the averaging of strengths and weaknesses. Instead of merely relying on composite scores, subtest analysis might be particularly meaningful to reach a better understanding of the areas of strength and weakness of the twice-exceptional population, who may not demonstrate evenly developed cognitive abilities but may show gifts in some areas of functioning while demonstrating difficulties in others. Research exploring the WISC subtest scatter of gifted students has typically noted a great amount of scatter among subtests (Patchett & Stansfield, 1992; Wilkinson, 1993).

Limited research has investigated the cognitive ability of gifted students with learning disabilities. Research examining the subtest scatter among gifted students with learning disabilities indicates that this group scores lowest on the subtests Arithmetic, Coding, Information, and Digit Span and highest on the subtests Information, Similarities, Vocabulary and Comprehension (Baum, Owen, & Dixon, 1991; Starnes, Ginevan, Stokes, & Barton, 1988). In addition, Barton and Starnes (1988) found that twice-exceptional students showed a greater amount of subtest scatter than the gifted group without learning disabilities, providing support for the heterogeneity of the twice-exceptional population. While no research has investigated the cognitive pattern of gifted students with behavioral or social-emotional difficulties, clinical studies investigating the cognitive profile of individuals with ADHD, ADD, or bipolar disorder revealed that these children demonstrate lower scores on the WISC-III Processing Speed and Freedom from Distractibility Indexes than the Verbal Comprehension and Perceptual Organization Index (Calhoun & Mayes, 2005).

Cluster analysis is a promising technique that could be used to identify a typology of twice-exceptionality based on cognitive abilities. Several studies have cluster analyzed the WISC scores of learning disabled individuals and consistently found between five and six distinguishable learning disability subtypes. No cluster analyses have been performed investigating the WISC subtypes of gifted or twice-exceptional children. However, based on the heterogeneity of the twice-exceptional population, cluster analysis might be a promising tool the understanding this understudied population. The identification of twice-exceptional subtypes may not only increase understanding of this group, but may also lead to more effective identification, classification, and treatment of this population. The purpose of this study was to explore the cognitive profiles of gifted children with learning, behavioral, and social-emotional difficulties. More specifically, this study investigated the ability scatter among twice-exceptional individuals to provide information about strengths and weaknesses of this group. In addition, based on the heterogeneity of this population, cluster analysis was used to discover specific subtype patterns present among twice-exceptional children and adolescents. Knowledge about the cognitive functioning of twice-exceptional children and adolescents will increase the understanding of this group, facilitate identification, reduce misdiagnosis, and aid in treatment and program planning of the twice-exceptional population.

Methods

Participants. Cases considered for inclusion in the study were drawn from an archival database of children and adolescents referred to a pediatric neuropsychologist specializing in twice-exceptional individuals. Children and adolescents were mainly referred due to concerns regarding their intellectual, emotional, social, behavioral, and sensory-motor functioning. Participants who met the following criteria were retained for inclusion in this study: (a) a WISC-IV Full Scale IQ of 120 or higher; (b) presence of a clinically significant learning disability, behavior problem, or social-emotional difficulty; and (c) age 6 years 0 months to 16 years 11 months. The final sample consisted of 95 participants (67 males, 28 females) between the ages of 6 and 16 years ($M = 10.29$, $SD = 2.94$). The ethnic background of the sample included: 86.3% White, 8.4% African American, 3.2% Latino, 1.1% Middle Eastern, and 1.1% Other.

Procedures. Participant data were derived from archival cases of neuropsychological evaluations conducted between 2004 and 2008. Measures were individually administered and scored according to standardized procedures by a licensed neuropsychologist. Test scores were obtained within the context of a comprehensive neuropsychological evaluation, which, in addition to the WISC, included several other measures depending on the specific referral question. Twice-exceptionality was assessed through clinical interview, behavioral observation, and the administration of a specific neuropsychological battery depending on the referral question. The battery included several of approximately 65 different measures used to assess the following domains of functioning: Intelligence and Cognitive/Mental Status (6), Achievement (2), Attention and Executive Functioning (8), Memory (7), Auditory Processing and Language (7), Sensory and Motor (13), Personality and Psychopathology (13), Motivation and Malingering (6), and Other (3).

The archival data utilized for this study consisted of the WISC-IV Full Scale IQ (FSIQ), factor index scores, mandatory subtest standard scores, and one supplementary subtest score (Information). Additional supplementary (optional) subtests were not utilized because they were not administered routinely and do not contribute to the computation of the IQ scores. In addition to the WISC-IV scores, demographic information including gender, age, and ethnicity was obtained about each student in the sample. All identifying information was removed to ensure confidentiality.

Measures. The WISC-IV (Wechsler, 2003) is the most recent revision of the WISC. It is an individually administered, comprehensive clinical instrument for assessing the intelligence of children ages 6.0 through 16.11 years. The WISC-IV standardization sample consisted of 2200 children stratified by age, sex, race, parent education, and geographic region based on data from the March 2000 U.S. Bureau of Census.

The internal consistency reliability coefficient for the WISC-IV FSIQ was .97 for all ages. The factor index scores, VCI, PRI, WMI, and PSI also have strong internal consistency reliability, with respective coefficients of .94, .92, .92, and .88. The internal consistency of the WISC-IV subtests ranged from .79 to .90, with the majority of subtests in the .80 to .89 range (Wechsler, 2003). The FSIQ test-retest stability coefficient of the WISC-IV was .89. Average test-retest stability coefficients for the four factor index scores include: .89 for VCI, .85 for PRI, .85 for WMI, and .79 for PSI. The average test-retest stability coefficient for the WISC-IV subtests ranged from .68 to .85 (Wechsler, 2003).

Data analysis. First, the performance of the entire sample of twice-exceptional children and adolescents on the WISC-IV was examined via the computation of means, standard deviations, and ranges for the WISC-IV FSIQ, VCI, PRI, WMI, PSI and the 11 subtest scores. A one-sample t test was used to compare the overall factor index score scatter present among the sample to the mean factor index score discrepancy found in the WISC-IV standardization sample. Additionally, the overall subtest score scatter obtained by the present sample was calculated and compared to the subtest score discrepancy found in the WISC-IV standardization sample, using a one-sample t test.

Second, this study aimed to identify the number of twice-exceptional subtypes on the WISC-IV. WISC-IV FSIQ, factor index, and subtest scores were submitted to a hierarchical agglomerative cluster analysis using Ward's (1963) minimum sum of squares method through SPSS (Norusis, 1995). This method is recommended based on research indicating that it is among the best performing hierarchical clustering algorithms and its effective use in previous WISC-III taxonomic research (Donders, 1996; Glutting, McDermott, Prifitera, & McGrath, 1994). Squared Euclidian distance was applied to the data as a similarity measure to estimate the number of clusters present in the sample. This method is recommended due to its sensitivity to the relative level, shape, and pattern of a given profile (Donders, 1996). The obtained cluster solution was compared on demographic information, including gender, age, and ethnicity. Chi-Square tests of independence were used to compare the different clusters based on gender and ethnicity. A one-way analysis of variance was performed to obtain the effect of mean ages on the different clusters.

Descriptive statistics, including mean and standard deviation for the FSIQ and four factor index scores were obtained for each of the clusters extracted through the hierarchical cluster analysis. Factor index score scatter obtained by each of the clusters was computed and compared to the mean scatter found in the WISC-IV standardization sample through the use of one-sample t tests. In addition, paired-samples t tests were used to determine whether any of the factor index scores obtained by a given cluster differed significantly from any others. In addition, descriptive statistics, including mean and standard deviation for the 11 subtest scores were calculated for each of the clusters. Subtest score discrepancies were computed and compared to the mean subtest scatter found in the WISC-IV standardization sample through the use of one-sample t tests. A multivariate analysis of variance (MANOVA) was used to determine whether the clusters differed from each other on any of the four factor index scores. Hotelling's T^2 was used to assess the statistical significance on the means of the four factor index scores between the different clusters. Crosstabulation was utilized to obtain the count and percentage of primary and secondary diagnoses present in each cluster.

Results

Descriptive sample statistics. The means, standard deviations, and ranges for the FSIQ, factor indices, and subtest scores of the WISC-IV for the entire sample are presented in Table 1. As a group, this clinic-referred sample obtained scores within the Superior range on the WISC-IV FSIQ ($M = 122.22$), within the Superior range on the VCI ($M = 127.51$) and PRI ($M = 121.28$), within the High Average range on the WMI ($M = 110.48$), and within the Average range on the PSI ($M = 103.08$). A substantial VCI > PSI discrepancy of 24.43 points and wide fluctuations in the subtest profile were evidenced by a range in mean scaled scores of 9.48 (Coding) to 15.34 (Similarities) within the sample.

The mean VCI > PSI discrepancy of 24.43 points attained by the twice-exceptional sample in the present study was compared to the discrepancy rate obtained by

Table 1

WISC-IV Full Scale IQ, Factor Index, and Subtest Scores for the Entire Sample (N = 95)

Area	Mean	SD	Range
Full Scale IQ	122.22	8.51	100-143
Factor Indices			
Verbal Comprehension	127.51	13.14	89-152
Perceptual Reasoning	121.28	10.37	100-143
Working Memory	110.48	13.52	83-146
Processing Speed	103.08	13.68	75-131
Subtest Scores			
Information	14.15	2.70	7-19
Similarities	15.34	2.32	10-22
Vocabulary	14.12	2.63	8-19
Comprehension	13.92	2.97	5-19
Block Design	12.88	2.79	5-19
Picture Concepts	13.19	2.66	6-19
Matrix Reasoning	14.00	2.54	8-19
Letter Number Sequencing	12.42	2.66	4-19
Digit Span	11.52	2.82	6-19
Symbol Search	11.40	2.45	5-18
Coding	9.48	2.85	2-18

Note. Full Scale IQ and Factor Index scores are reported as standard scores, $M = 100$, $SD = 15$. Subtest scores are reported as standard scores, $M = 10$, $SD = 3$.

the WISC-IV standardization sample. According to the WISC-IV manual Table B.2., a VCI > PSI discrepancy of 24 points or more occurred in 14.6% of the standardization sample (FSIQ > 120; Wechsler, 2003, p. 262). Further, a VCI > PSI discrepancy of 40 points or more occurred in 2% of the standardization sample (FSIQ > 120; Wechsler, 2003, p. 262), while the same discrepancy occurred in 22.1% of the twice-exceptional sample. Thus, a 40-point discrepancy was approximately 11 times more common in the twice-exceptional sample compared to the standardization sample of children and adolescents with an FSIQ > 120, a statistically significant difference ($t = 10.82$; $p > .001$). In addition, subtest scatter obtained by the twice-exceptional sample was compared to the amount of scatter required for statistical significance. The 5.86 point Similarities-Coding discrepancy obtained was compared to the WISC-IV manual Table B.3, which indicated that a Similarities-Coding discrepancy of 3.23 points is considered to be statistically significant at the .05 level (Wechsler, 2003).

Identification and validation of a WISC-IV typology. A hierarchical agglomerative cluster analysis was used to investigate the number of twice-exceptional clusters that emerged from profiles based on a frequently used ability instrument. This technique formed a similarity-dissimilarity matrix within which the similarity between each case was described and then gradually built clusters through agglomerative techniques until similar cases were put into the same clusters. Squared Euclidean distances were used as similarity measures due to their high sensitivity to the relative level, shape, and pattern of a given profile (Aldenderfer & Blashfield, 1984). Ward's (1963) minimum variance method was the hierarchical agglomerative cluster technique to complete the analysis, as this method was designed to generate clusters that minimize the variance within them and maximize the homogeneity of cases within each group.

Sixteen cognitive variables were used in the cluster analysis, including the FSIQ, the four factor index scores, and 11 subtest scores (the 10 core subtest scores and Information) of the WISC-IV. Prior to conducting a cluster analysis, the completeness of the data matrix was considered by searching the data for missing cases. For the current data set, no missing variables were present; therefore, no data imputation methods were needed. Because the present sample was thought to be characterized by heterogeneity, outliers were considered part of the target population and retained for further analysis. Cluster analysis of all 95 cases yielded 1 to 10 clusters and a 7-cluster solution was selected upon an inspection and comparison of corresponding cluster memberships, descriptive statistics, and interrelationships (Huberty, DiStefano, & Kamphaus, 1997). A 7-cluster solution was found to be the most robust and meaningful in terms of clinical relevance and discernibility of clusters. Means and standard deviations were computed for the WISC-IV FSIQ, factor index, and subtest scores of each of the seven clusters. A graphic display of the seven clusters based on factor indices is presented in Figure 1, whereas Tables 2 and 3 provide the specific descriptive statistics for the FSIQ, factor index, and subtest scores.

To validate this cluster solution, the characteristics of the clusters on other variables that were not included in the clustering process were then considered, including gender, ethnicity, and age. No statistically significant differences ($p > .10$) between clusters were found based on gender [$\chi^2(6) = 9.21$, ns] and ethnicity [$\chi^2(18) = 11.18$, ns] (see Table 4). However, a one-way ANOVA performed on the effect of mean ages was significant [$F(6, 88) = 3.048, p = .009$]. Multiple comparisons of each group indicated that the mean age of participants in Cluster 6 (11.92 years) was significantly higher than the mean age of those in Cluster 4 (7.38 years). Table 5 presents the mean ages for

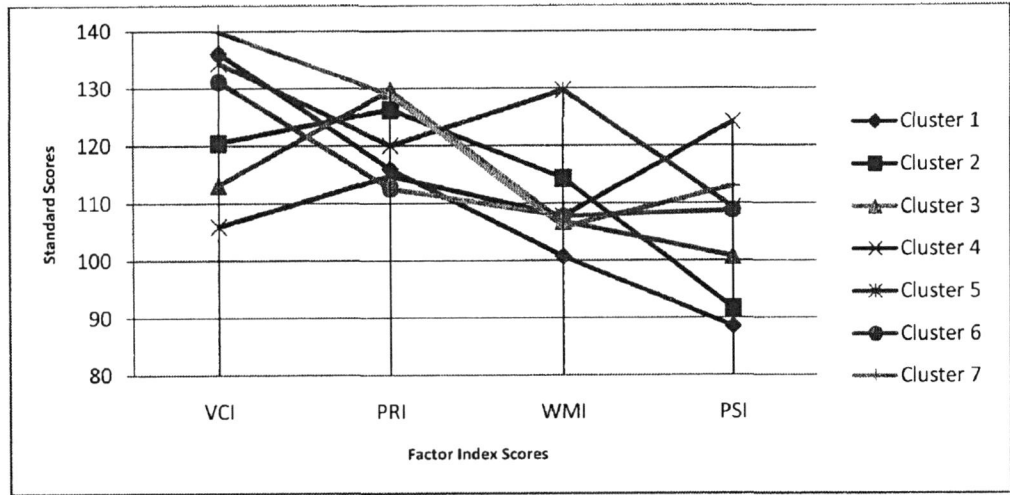

Note. VCI = Verbal Comprehension Index; PRI = Perceptual Reasoning Index; WMI = Working Memory Index; PSI = Processing Speed Index. Factor Index scores are reported as standard scores, $M = 100, SD = 15$.

Figure 1. WISC-IV factor index score profiles for the seven WISC-IV cluster subtypes.

Table 2

Mean Full Scale and Factor Index Scores and Standard Deviations for the Seven Cluster Subtypes

Cluster	FSIQ M	SD	VCI M	SD	PRI M	SD	WMI M	SD	PSI M	SD
1	117.44	7.08	136.11	6.31	115.94	10.19	100.67	8.58	88.56	9.43
2	118.73	8.80	120.47	9.05	126.27	8.69	114.33	12.77	91.67	9.40
3	119.15	5.08	113.15	7.05	129.62	3.20	106.77	13.77	100.69	7.66
4	116.50	6.44	105.88	10.30	114.75	8.88	107.75	14.61	124.12	4.09

TWICE-EXCEPTIONAL

5	131.47	7.75	134.40	7.75	120.00	11.77	129.60	6.77	109.27	10.32
6	120.69	2.50	131.08	4.87	112.54	5.09	107.69	3.84	108.77	5.12
7	130.31	4.23	139.85	7.00	128.85	6.30	105.77	9.10	113.00	6.89

Note. Population standard scores $M = 100$ and $SD = 15$ for all variables. FSIQ = Full Scale Intelligent Quotient; VCI = Verbal Comprehension Index; PRI = Perceptual Reasoning Index; WMI = Working Memory Index; PSI = Processing Speed Index.

Table 3

Mean Subtest Scores and Standard Deviations for the Seven Cluster Subtypes

Variables	1		2		3		4		5		6		7	
	M	SD	M	SD	M	SD	M	SD	M	SD	M	SD	M	SD
IN	15.22	2.10	12.67	1.68	12.15	2.64	11.13	2.90	15.60	2.44	14.62	1.98	16.08	1.71
SI	16.56	1.92	14.47	1.89	12.85	1.57	13.00	1.77	16.53	1.55	15.62	2.22	16.92	1.66
VO	5.56	1.76	12.73	1.87	11.54	1.71	10.62	1.85	15.93	2.25	14.08	1.50	16.38	1.50
CO	15.11	3.51	13.27	2.43	12.62	1.76	9.62	2.72	13.93	1.39	14.85	2.51	16.00	2.48
PCn	12.67	2.22	13.80	2.51	14.92	2.22	11.12	3.14	12.87	3.50	12.54	2.30	13.77	1.70
MR	12.83	2.90	14.87	2.03	15.38	1.90	13.12	1.46	14.33	2.16	12.15	2.70	15.23	2.32
LN	10.83	1.72	13.27	2.76	11.77	3.14	12.00	3.07	15.07	2.63	12.00	1.08	11.92	1.80
DS	9.72	2.08	11.93	2.43	10.92	3.01	11.00	3.12	15.07	2.40	11.15	1.41	10.69	1.84
SS	9.28	1.53	9.73	2.25	10.69	1.55	14.38	2.72	12.40	2.17	12.15	.80	13.23	1.64
CD	6.72	2.24	7.40	1.64	9.38	1.66	14.00	2.51	10.67	2.38	10.77	1.36	10.38	1.94

Note. Population standard scores $M = 10$ and $SD = 3$ for all variables. IN = Information; SI = Similarities; VO = Vocabulary; CO = Comprehension; BD = Block Design; PCn = Picture Concept; MR = Matrix Reasoning; LN = Letter Number Sequencing; DS = Digit Span; SS = Symbol Search; CD = Coding.

Table 4

Frequency of Gender and Ethnicity (Percentage) for the Seven WISC-IV Cluster Subtypes

Variable	1	2	3	4	5	6	7
Gender (%)							
Male	83.3	80.0	46.2	50.0	73.3	61.5	84.6
Female	16.7	20.0	53.8	50.0	26.7	38.5	15.4
Ethnicity (%)							
Caucasian	88.9	86.7	91.7	75.0	80.0	92.3	92.3
African Am.	5.6	13.3	8.3	12.5	6.7	7.7	7.7
Latino	5.6	.0	.0	12.5	6.7	.0	.0
Middle Eastern	.0	.0	.0	.0	6.7	.0	.0

children in the seven clusters. This finding indicates that children in Cluster 4 may be referred at a younger age, while children in Cluster 6 tend to get referred at a later age. This may suggest that a developmental trend exists in terms of initial referral and diagnosis of a given subtype of twice-exceptional children. Future studies could further examine such developmental trends.

Table 5

Mean Ages and Ranges in Years for Each Cluster

Cluster	n	M	SD	Range
1	18	10.23	2.49	6-15
2	15	10.87	3.25	7-16
3	13	8.92	2.81	6-13
4	8	7.38	1.51	6-11
5	15	11.00	3.21	7-16
6	13	11.92	2.57	9-16
7	13	10.38	2.66	6-16

Inspection of Figure 1 and Table 2 indicates that the seven clusters were differentiated primarily by level of performance on VCI, PRI, WMI, and PSI scores. Descriptive labels were assigned to the seven clusters based on the most salient features of each profile.

Cluster 1: Verbal Learners ($n = 18$). This cluster was composed of children and adolescents who had particularly low processing speed abilities, while showing very superior verbal abilities. The subgroup attained WISC-IV factor index scores that were within the Low Average to Very Superior range. The group of Verbal Learners showed the following factor sequence: VCI > PRI > WMI > PSI (See Table 2), with a VCI > PSI discrepancy of 47.55 points, which is more than triple the mean VCI > PSI discrepancy of 12.9 in the normal population ($110 < FSIQ < 119$) and is significantly greater than the normative mean at the .001 level ($t = 10.80$). All factor scores were found to differ significantly from all others. An examination of the subtest scores obtained by the Verbal Learners showed that children in this group scored highest on Similarities (16.56) and lowest on Coding (6.72) subtests, with a range of 9.84 points. The scaled-score range of 9.84 earned by the Verbal Learners is slightly more than one standard deviation above the range of 7.0 for the normal population, a significant difference ($t = 3.37; p < .005$).

Cluster 2: Attention Difficulty ($n = 15$). Cluster 2 was composed of children and adolescents who demonstrated processing speed at the very low end of the average range. The Attention Difficulty group showed the following factor sequence: PRI > VCI > WMI > PSI (See Table 2), with an overall scatter of 34.60 points. The mean PRI > PSI discrepancy of 34.60 points attained by the Attention Difficulty group is more than double the mean PRI > PSI discrepancy of 12.7 points obtained in the normal population (110 < FSIQ < 119) and is significantly greater than the normative mean at the .001 level ($t = 7.81$). Ninety-five percent Bonferroni confidence intervals were used to determine whether any of the factor scores obtained by the group differed significantly from any others. Findings indicated that children in the Attention Difficulty group scored significantly higher on PRI than VCI ($t = 2.26; p < 0.05$), significantly higher on VCI than PSI ($t = 14.66; p < .001$), significantly higher on PRI than WMI ($t = 2.57, p < .05$), significantly higher on PRI than PSI ($t = 12.34, p < .001$), and significantly higher on WMI than PSI ($t = 5.13, p < .001$), while there was no significant difference between VCI and WMI scores. In addition, children in this group scored highest on Matrix Reasoning (14.87) and lowest on Coding (7.40) subtests, obtaining a scatter of 7.47 points, which is only slightly above the mean range of 7.0 for the normal population and does not constitute a significant difference.

Cluster 3: Visual-spatial learners ($n = 13$). The third cluster is characterized by children and adolescents with superior perceptual abilities. The subgroup attained WISC-IV factor index scores that were within the Average to Superior range, with the following factor sequence: PRI > VCI > WMI > PSI (see Table 2). The Visual-Spatial Learners displayed a PRI > PSI scatter of 28.93, a discrepancy that is approximately double the value of 12.7 in the normal population and is significantly greater than the normative mean at the .001 level ($t = 9.26$). A comparison of factor scores within the group of Visual-Spatial Learners indicated that the group performed significantly higher on PRI than on VCI ($t = 6.75; p < .001$), significantly higher on VCI than PSI ($t = 3.85, p < .05$), significantly higher on PRI than WMI ($t = 6.42, p < .001$), significantly higher on PRI than PSI ($t = 16.51, p < .001$), and significantly higher on WMI than PSI ($t = 2.26, p < .05$), while there was no significant difference between VCI and WMI scores. In addition, an examination of the subtest scores obtained by the Visual-Spatial Learners indicated that children in this group scored highest on Matrix Reasoning (15.38) and lowest on Coding (9.38) subtests, with a range of 6.0 points, which does not differ significantly from the subtest range of 7 points found in the normal population.

Cluster 4: Quick performers ($n = 8$). The fourth cluster consists of children and adolescents with superior processing speed and average verbal abilities. Quick Performers showed WISC-IV factor index scores within the Average to Superior range, obtaining the following factor sequence: PSI > PRI > WMI > VCI (See Table 2). The group displayed a PSI > VCI scatter of 18.24, a discrepancy that does not differ significantly from the normative mean ($110 < FSIQ < 119$) of 11.5. An examination of factor scores within the group of Quick Performers indicated that the group performed significantly higher on PSI than VCI ($t = 5.24, p < .05$), significantly higher on PSI than PRI ($t = 2.51, p < .05$), and significantly higher on PSI than WMI ($t = 2.98, p < .05$), while there was no significant difference between VCI and PRI, VCI and WMI, and PRI and WMI scores. An inspection of the subtest scores obtained by the Quick Performers showed that children in this group scored highest on Symbol Search (14.38) and lowest on Comprehension (9.62) subtests, a discrepancy that does not differ significantly from the standardization sample.

Cluster 5: Accelerated learners ($n = 15$). The fifth cluster is composed of children and adolescents with superior working memory and very superior verbal abilities. The subgroup attained WISC-IV factor index scores within the Average to Very Superior range, showing the following factor sequence: VCI > WMI > PRI > PSI (see Table 2). Accelerated Learners displayed a mean VCI > PSI scatter of 25.13, a discrepancy that is approximately 1.5 times the mean VCI > PSI scatter of 15.7 attained in the normal population (FSIQ > 120) and is significantly greater than the normative mean ($t = 2.54; p < .05$). A comparison of factor scores within the group of Accelerated Learners indicated that these children and adolescents performed significantly higher on VCI than PRI ($t = 3.98; p = .001$), significantly higher on VCI than PSI ($t = 6.77, p < .001$), significantly higher on WMI than PRI ($t = 3.24, p < .05$), significantly higher on PRI than PSI ($t = 4.57, p < .001$), and significantly higher on WMI than PSI ($t = 6.71, p < .001$), while there was no significant difference between VCI and WMI scores. In addition, Accelerated Learners scored highest on Similarities (16.53) and lowest on Coding (10.67) subtests, with a range of 5.86 points, which does not differ significantly from the mean subtest scatter range of 7.0 points obtained by the normal population.

Cluster 6: Nonverbal learning weakness ($n = 13$). The sixth cluster includes children and adolescents with very superior verbal abilities and lower nonverbal scores. This subgroup obtained WISC-IV factor index scores within the Average to Very Superior range and showed the following factor sequence: VCI > PRI > PSI > WMI (see Table 2). The Nonverbal Learning Weakness group displayed a VCI > WMI scatter of 23.39 points, a discrepancy that is about 1.5 times the value of 13.9 in the normal population (FSIQ > 120) and is significantly greater than the normative mean at the .001 level ($t = 4.53$). An examination of factor scores within the Nonverbal Learning Weakness group indicated that the group scored significantly higher on VCI than PRI ($t = 9.31; p < .001$), significantly higher on VCI than WMI ($t = 11.16, p < .001$), significantly higher on VCI than PSI ($t = 9.03, p < .001$), and significantly higher on PRI than WMI ($t = 2.69, p < .05$), while there was no significant difference between PRI and PSI, and WMI and PSI scores. The Nonverbal Learning Weakness group scored highest on Comprehension (14.85) and lowest on Coding (10.77) subtests, with a range of 4.08 points, which is about one standard deviation below the mean range of 7.0 for the normal population, a significant difference ($t = -3.67; p < .05$).

Cluster 7: High general ability ($n = 13$). The seventh cluster is composed of children and adolescents with specific verbal and perceptual strengths. The High General Ability group earned WISC-IV factor index scores within the Average to Very Superior range, displaying the following factor sequence: VCI > PRI > PSI > WMI (see Table 2). The High General Ability group displayed a VCI > WMI scatter of 34.08 points, a discrepancy that is almost 2.5 times the value of 13.9 in the normal population and is significantly greater than the normative mean ($t = 8.27; p < .001$). An examination of factor index scores within the group indicated that all comparisons were statistically significant. Children and adolescents in the High General Ability group scored significantly higher on VCI than PRI ($t = 4.23; p = .001$), significantly higher on VCI than WMI ($t = 13.97; p < 0.001$), significantly higher on VCI than PSI ($t = 8.00, p < .001$), significantly higher on PRI than WMI ($t = 6.42, p < .001$), significantly higher on

PRI than PSI ($t = 6.77$, $p < .001$), and significantly higher on PSI than WMI ($t = 2.23$, $p < .05$). Moreover, children and adolescents in the High Ability group scored highest on Similarities (16.92) and lowest on Coding (10.38) subtests, with a range of 6.54 points, which does not differ significantly from the mean subtest range of 7.0 obtained by the normal population.

Comparisons were made through a MANOVA to determine whether the seven subtypes differed from each other on any of the factor index scores. Hotelling's T^2 was used to assess the statistical significance on the means of the four indices between the seven subtypes. Results from the MANOVA revealed significant differences between the subtypes [$F(24, 334) = 21.35$, $p < .001$]. Post hoc comparisons indicated that on the VCI, the Verbal Learners subtype obtained a significantly higher score relative to the Attention Difficulty, Visual-Spatial Learners, and Quick Performers subtypes ($p < .001$). The Attention Difficulty subtype showed a significantly higher score on VCI than the Quick Performers while obtaining lower scores on VCI than the Accelerated Learners, the Nonverbal Learning Weakness, and the High General Ability subtypes ($p < .01$). The Visual-Spatial Learners subtype demonstrated significantly lower scores on VCI than the Accelerated Learners, the Nonverbal Learning Weakness and the High General Ability subtypes ($p < .001$). The Quick Performers subtype showed significantly lower scores on VCI than the Accelerated Learners, the Nonverbal Learning Weakness, and the High General Ability subtypes ($p < .001$).

On the PRI index, the Verbal Learners subtype showed significantly lower scores than the Attention Difficulty, the Visual-Spatial Learners, and the High General Ability subtypes ($p < .05$). The Attention Difficulty subtype demonstrated significantly higher scores on PRI than the Quick Performers and the Nonverbal Learning Weakness subtypes ($p < .05$). The Visual-Spatial Learners showed significantly higher scores on PRI than Quick Performers and the Nonverbal Learning Weakness subtypes ($p < .05$). The Quick Performers obtained a significantly higher PRI score than the High General Ability subtype ($p < .05$). The Nonverbal Learning Weakness subtype showed a significantly lower PRI score than the High General Ability subtype ($p < .001$).

On the WMI, the Accelerated Learners subtype obtained significantly higher scores than all other groups ($p < .005$). In addition, the Attention Difficulty subtype scored significantly higher on WMI than the Verbal Learners ($p = .005$). On the PSI, the Verbal Learners scored significantly lower than the Visual-Spatial Learners, the Quick Performers, the Accelerated Learners, the Nonverbal Learning Weakness, and the High General Ability subtypes ($p < .005$), while there was no significant difference to the Attention Difficulty subtype. The Attention Difficulty subtype showed significantly lower scores on PSI than the Quick Performers, the Accelerated Learners, the Nonverbal Learning Weakness, and the High General Ability subtypes ($p < .001$). The Visual-Spatial Learners subtype scored significantly lower on PSI than the Quick Performers and the High General Ability subtypes ($p < .005$). The Quick Performers showed a significantly higher PSI than the Nonverbal Learning Weakness subtype ($p = .002$). Primary and secondary diagnoses of the seven subtypes are summarized in Tables 6 and 7.

Discussion

The purpose of this study was to identify the cognitive pattern of twice-exceptional children and adolescents to reveal the pattern of abilities present in this heterogeneous group. The WISC-IV full-scale IQ, factor index, and subtest score patterns of twice-exceptional students were identified and validated. A cluster analysis on the entire sample of twice-exceptional students confirmed the heterogeneity of this group, indicating seven reliable subtypes that were differentiated primarily by level of performance on the four factor index scores. These were: (a) Verbal Learners, (b) Attention Difficulty, (c) Visual-Spatial Learners, (d) Quick Performers, (e) Accelerated Learners, (f) Nonverbal Learning Weakness, and (g) High General Ability.

The overall sample of twice-exceptional children and adolescents assessed in this study obtained a factor score sequence of VCI > PRI > WMI > and PSI, which is consistent with the factor sequence observed in the WISC-IV validity study of gifted

Table 6

Primary Diagnoses (Count and Percentage) of the Seven Clusters

Diagnosis	1	2	3	4	5	6	7
ADHD	17(94.4%)	15(100%)	7(53.8%)	7(87.5%)	10(66.7%)	9(69.2%)	8(61.5%)
Learning Disorder			3(23.1%)				
Cognitive Disorder			1(7.7%)				
Anxiety Disorder			2(15.4%)	1(12.5%)	3(20.0%)	3(23.1%)	5(38.5%)
ODD					2(13.3%)		
Depression	1 (5.6%)						
PDD							1(7.7%)

Note. ADHD = attention deficit hyperactivity disorder, ODD = oppositional defiant disorder, PDD = pervasive developmental disorder.

Table 7

Secondary Diagnoses (Count and Percentage) of the Seven Clusters

Diagnosis	1	2	3	4	5	6	7
Learning Disorder	3(16.6%)	1(6.7%)		4(50%)	1(6.7%)		1(7.7%)
Anxiety Disorder	3(16.6%)	2(13.3%)			1(6.7%)		1(7.7%)
ODD	1(5.6%)		2(15.4%)				
PDD	1(5.6%)				1(6.7%)	1(7.7%)	

Note. ADHD = attention deficit hyperactivity disorder, ODD = oppositional defiant disorder, PDD = pervasive developmental disorder.

children. Overall, the sample of twice-exceptional children and adolescents showed strengths on VCI and PRI compared to lower WMI and PSI scores, which is consistent with research findings on the strengths and weaknesses of gifted children without disabilities (Wechsler, 2003). It has been argued that the two larger VCI and PRI factors are more psychometrically robust, have stronger construct validity, and are more g loaded than the WMI and PSI factors (Flanagan & Kaufman, 2004). The overall PSI weakness observed in this sample of twice-exceptional children and adolescents is consistent with a PSI weakness among gifted students that has been

noted in previous research. For example, the validity studies of the WISC-III and WISC-IV with gifted children both indicated that this group performed lowest on PSI (Wechsler, 2003; Wechsler, 1991). In addition, the twice-exceptional group as a whole showed strengths and weaknesses in the same subtests noted for the gifted population. The twice-exceptional sample scored highest on the Similarities subtest (15.34) and lowest on the subtests Coding (9.48) and Symbol Search (11.40) (Fishkin, Kampsnider, & Pack, 1996; Patchett & Stanfield, 1992; Wilkinson, 1993).

Overall, the sample displayed a substantial mean VCI > PSI discrepancy of 24.43 points, and 22.1% of the sample demonstrated a VCI > PSI discrepancy of 40 points or more, a scatter obtained by only 2% of individuals in the WISC-IV standardization sample who display an FSIQ of 120 or higher. This highlights that the twice-exceptional group exhibited a factor index score discrepancy which is significant and unusual in the normal population. The significant scatter present among factor index and subtest scores of twice-exceptional students found in this study continues to highlight the importance of inspecting the profile of strengths and weaknesses of this group rather than relying on the mathematically derived full scale IQ score. To obtain a true understanding of twice-exceptional students, their discrete sets of abilities need to be analyzed separately rather than averaged into a misleading full scale IQ score. However, because placement in programs frequently continues to be dependent on Full Scale IQ scores, many twice-exceptional students with uneven patterns are denied differentiated programming due to an averaging of extremely discrepant scores. To address this problem, an inspection of ability patterns is highly recommended to better serve this population. Performance on subtest and factor scores on the WISC-IV provides valuable diagnostic information that has clinical and instructional implications.

Cluster 1. The Verbal Learner subtype demonstrated the largest factor scatter among all clusters with a VCI > PSI discrepancy of 47.55 points. Moreover, significant discrepancies were found among all four factor index scores, with the following factor sequence VCI > PRI > WMI > PSI. The group's significantly higher (over 1 SD) language/verbal abilities (VCI) compared to their visual processing abilities (PRI) has a number of implications for their overall thinking style and emotional well-being. In general, these children and adolescents process, learn, and perform best with oral language. Thus, this group shows strengths in the processing of words and language-based meanings; listening to, keeping pace with, and following verbal sequences; processing verbal meanings and implications; and simultaneously formulating verbal responses. However, when presented with visual information, Verbal Learners require more time and cognitive resources to complete the steps from input to output of information. In addition, children and adolescents with strong verbal and weak visual abilities also tend toward linear, concrete, and detail thinking vs. non-linear, abstract, and gist thinking. In addition, the group's comparably low processing speed ability makes their profile particularly problematic. Based on their PSI weakness, these students demonstrate visual and motor difficulties, such as poor fine-motor skills and difficulties with hand-eye coordination that likely affect their performance in several areas, including writing and math. Thus, the slow speed of these students is likely experienced as a handicap by them, which can cause frustration and lead to reduced self-esteem. To reduce frustration among this group, it is important that these children and adolescents receive adequate praise and support for their efforts to make them more tolerant of their slow speed. An additional avenue that can help this group succeed is the use of technology, which can enable Verbal Learners to become more successful learners by accessing and organizing information and improving the visual quality of their finished products.

Cluster 2. Children and adolescents in the Attention Difficulty cluster demonstrate less factor scatter, with the exception of PSI, which was a relative weakness for this group. With the exception of PSI, the factor profile of this subtype shows less scatter (PRI-VCI = 11.94 points), suggesting that individuals in this group are quite capable and likely demonstrate less concurrent frustration, and mood and self-esteem problems than Verbal Learners. If mood or self-esteem problems are experienced by this group, then such problems are likely to be less intense and impacting. While the Attention Difficulty subtype is likely to generally perform well in the classroom, individuals in cluster two show difficulties with processing speed. Processing speed requires little complex thinking or mental processing, but instead includes simple, clerical type tasks. These students may struggle with their ability to fluently and automatically perform cognitive tasks, especially when under pressure to maintain focused attention and concentration. It is noteworthy that all individuals in the Attention Difficulty subtype carried a primary diagnosis of ADHD, which has further implications for this group of students. These children are highly focused when engaged in areas of strength and interest (i.e., experienced as highly stimulating) while struggling to maintain focus on activities that are experienced as boring or repetitive (Baum et al., 1995). To support their ability to sustain attention, it is recommended that educators develop curricula that are engaging. This can be accomplished by utilizing an interest-based curriculum or creating entry points to curriculum based on a student's unique profile of talents (Gardner, 1999).

Cluster 3. Visual-Spatial Learners show a strong ability on tasks that require visual perception, organization and reasoning with visually presented, nonverbal material to solve problems that are not typically taught in school. Based on their lower VCI

(113.15) vs. PRI (129.62) score, Visual-Spatial Learners may tend to understand overall concepts, but may struggle with their articulation. These students tend to see the big picture, but may miss the details. Their learning occurs in a holistic all-or-none-fashion rather than in the typical step-by-step manner in which most teachers teach. Strategies that are particularly helpful in teaching students with visual-spatial strengths include: using visual aids, such as overhead projectors, and visual imagery in lectures; using manipulative material to allow hands-on experience; using a sight approach to reading rather than phonics; using a visualization approach to spelling; avoiding rote memorization and instead using more conceptual or inductive approaches; avoiding drill and repetition; and engaging students in independent studies or group projects that involve problem-finding as well as problem-solving (Silverman, 1989).

Cluster 4. Quick Performers perform at high speed, demonstrating strengths in performing somewhat boring clerical type tasks faster. However, some of their skills, particularly language-based abilities, are actually less well developed. Based on their relatively low scores on VCI (105.88) and their average to high average scores on WMI (107.75) and PRI (114.76), it may be questionable whether this group meets qualifications for giftedness in a more traditional sense. Based on their score profile, this group of children and adolescents shows lower complexity of thoughts, problem-solving ability, and ability to integrate more complex information. Given that all individuals in this subtype suffered from either ADHD or Anxiety Disorder, it is possible that the high PSI score found in this group is coupled with impulsivity. Thus, these children and adolescents may have a tendency to move very fast out of their impulsivity.

Consequently, their propensity for tasks that require speed may not necessarily be a strength, because it may lead to less focus on details and mistakes. While Quick Performers demonstrate Processing Speed strengths, individuals in this group tend to struggle with verbal communication and working memory. To address the weaknesses of this group, visual and kinesthetic experiences used to convey abstract ideas may be helpful. This accommodation removes the stumbling block of verbal communication and allows the visual image to guide the mental processes.

Cluster 5. Accelerated Learners show strong abilities utilizing verbal information and have a well-developed ability to apprehend and hold information in immediate awareness. They have a tendency to easily acquire new information, integrate it with previously learned facts, and then move it into storage. They easily follow verbal or written directions, process auditory information, organize thoughts for speaking and writing, and learn multi-step procedures. While Accelerated Learners demonstrate a relatively evenly developed profile, they performed somewhat lower on processing speed, which might be exhibited by motor difficulties and a hand-eye coordination weakness. However, while this group demonstrates a relative PSI weakness, index score scatter is in the *average* range and is therefore likely experienced as less debilitating. Based on the fairly evenly developed profile of this group, these students likely experience less frustration and can find a state of *best fit* for their learning, with a comparatively minimal amount of learning difficulties. To support the learning of this group, it is recommended that interventions use the strong working memory and verbal skills of this group. A stimulating classroom environment that encourages the intrinsic motivation of Accelerated Learners is highly recommended to reduce boredom in this group.

Cluster 6. Students in the Nonverbal Learning Weakness subtype are likely to speak eloquently and have a well-developed vocabulary. These students are likely to be top readers, achieve excellent spelling scores, and express themselves articulately. Based on their profile, these individuals may excel during the primary years when the building blocks for learning are formed, such as learning rote facts, or reading accurately out loud. However, as these children and adolescents get older, areas of weakness are likely to exert growing influences on the academic achievement of this group, and they may increasingly experience processing difficulties that resemble or meet criteria for a nonverbal learning disability. Children with nonverbal learning weakness may struggle getting the gist of things and understanding things at a conceptual level. They have difficulty organizing the visual-spatial field, adapting to new or novel situations, and accurately reading nonverbal signals or cues. Concurrent with increasing academic difficulties, students with nonverbal learning weakness may experience more anxiety and social difficulties as they get older. Based on the fact that academic performance likely becomes difficult for this group as academic demands increase, recognizing the ability discrepancy of students with nonverbal learning weakness and employing interventions early in their schooling become important to maximize academic success and reduce the risk of social-emotional problems.

Cluster 7. Children and adolescents in the High General Ability subtype have very robust verbal and nonverbal intellectual skills and have a high potential to succeed in the classroom. High General Ability students easily process verbal meanings and implications, follow verbal sequences, and formulate verbal responses. They show a strong ability in processing, organizing, and reasoning with visually presented nonverbal material and easily solve tasks that cannot be performed automatically. While individuals in the High General Ability subtype are very bright, they show some difficulty in the areas of working memory and processing speed, which makes it difficult for these students to hold variables in mind while processing information. These students likely come across to others as being very capable, and their struggles in the areas of working memory and processing speed may be perceived as a surprise. Thus, there is the risk that these students get shamed because parents and teachers do not understand their weaknesses and believe that these students simply say things to get out of trouble, when in actuality students in the High General Ability subtype are bad problem-solvers in real time. Teaching to the verbal and visual reasoning strengths of the High General Ability group while bypassing, compensating for, and remediating the working memory and performance speed weaknesses of this group is recommended.

Implications. Twice-exceptional children and adolescents present a paradoxical picture of exceptional strengths coexisting with specific deficits. These students may use their gifts and talents to compensate for their deficits and overcome their academic difficulties with support, understanding, and instructional interventions and accommodations. However, because these students are frequently able to utilize their strengths to compensate for their weaker areas, deficits commonly remain unrecognized, misunderstood, and underserved. Consequently, diagnosticians, including psychologists, audiologists, optometrists, and occupational therapists need to be aware of the compensatory behaviors this group may employ and inspect how their weaker areas compare to their stronger areas. Likewise, it is important to recognize that among twice-exceptional children with high abilities in certain areas, scores in the average range on the WISC-IV may be sufficient to indicate a deficit. While an average score does not constitute a deficit when compared to the population in general, it can indicate a significant personal weakness compared to the student's abilities in other areas.

It is hoped that the seven twice-exceptional subtypes identified in the present study will facilitate educational decisions being rendered for this population. The appropriate identification of strengths and weaknesses allows twice-exceptional children and adolescents to benefit from educational programs that are flexible and individualized to their specific needs. More specifically, education programs should foster the talents of this group, provide developmental instruction in areas of average growth and offer remedial and adaptive teaching in areas of deficits. In addition, as is true for all children with special needs, including the gifted and twice-exceptional populations, early intervention provides the best opportunity for optimal development (Silverman, 1998). Thus, as early as during the preschool and primary years, twice-exceptional students would benefit from a curriculum that nurtures their strengths, while accommodating for their areas of weakness. A comprehensive program should provide a learning environment valuing individual talents, educational support including compensatory strategies for areas of weakness, and school-based counseling services to address the mix of talents and weaknesses this group experiences (NAGC, 1998).

Limitations. There are a number of possible limitations in this study that should be considered when interpreting the results. First of all, participants included individuals referred for comprehensive neuropsychological testing, which may have biased the sample toward relatively more severe symptomatology. Consequently, the degree to which the findings will generalize to samples of non-referred twice-exceptional children and adolescents is unknown. Also, the sample sizes of some of the seven clusters were relatively low; and the majority of children and adolescents in the present sample were male (83.3%) and White (88.9%). Consequently, findings may not generalize to more diverse samples of twice-exceptional students. A further limitation of this study is that it does not establish the diagnostic utility of the extracted profiles. Diagnostic utility needs to be established through demonstrating that the subtypes prescribe useful interventions or predict future outcomes. It is suggested that future research attempt to replicate the seven twice-exceptional subtypes extracted in the current study and identify potentially helpful interventions for the different subtypes.

Future research. Future research should attempt to validate the seven twice-exceptional subtypes extracted in the present study through replication in an independent sample. Studies should focus on including a diverse sample in terms of gender, ethnicity, and geographic location. Replication of the cluster solution identified in the current study will lend support toward the reliability and validity of the seven twice-exceptional profiles. Questions of treatment responsiveness and more complete neuropsychological functioning profiles also merit consideration. An additional area for future research is the exploration of overlap between identified subtypes with specific diagnostic groups, such as ADHD, LD, or Asperger's Disorder. Findings suggest that certain diagnoses (e.g., ADHD) appear to be more common among certain cluster subtypes. It is recommended that future research investigate more closely the presentation and overlap of diagnoses. Future research might examine the diagnostic utility of the subtypes identified in this study by investigating whether subtypes prescribe useful interventions or predict future outcomes.

References

Aldenderfer, M. S., & Blashfield, R. K. (1984). *Cluster analysis.* Newbury Park, CA: Sage Publications.

Barton, J. M., & Starnes, W. T. (1988). Identifying distinguishing characteristics of gifted and talented/learning disabled students. *Roeper Review, 12*(1), 23-29.

Barton, J. M., & Starnes, W. T. (1989). Identifying distinguishing characteristics of gifted and talented/learning disabled students. *Roeper Review, 12*(1), 23-29.

Baum, S., Owen, S. V., & Dixon, J. (1991). *To be gifted and learning disabled: From definitions to practical intervention strategies.* Mansfield Center, CT: Creative Learning Press.

Brody, L. E., & Mills, C. J. (1997). Gifted children with learning disabilities: A review of the issues. *Journal of Learning Disabilities, 30*(3), 282-296.

Calhoun, S. L., & Mayes, S. D. (2005). Processing speed in children with clinical disorders. *Psychology in the Schools, 42*, 333-343.

Donders, J. (1996). Cluster subtypes in the WISC-III standardization sample: Analysis of factor index scores. *Psychological Assessment, 8*(3), 312-318.

Fishkin, A. S., Kampsnider, J. J., & Pack, L. (1996). Exploring the WISC-III as a measure of giftedness. *Roeper Review, 18*(3), 226-231.

Flanagan, D. P., & Kaufman, A. S. (2004). *Essentials of WISC-IV assessment.* Hoboken, NJ: John Wiley & Sons.

Fox, L. H. (1983). Gifted students with reading problems. In L. H. Fox, L. Brody, & D. Tobin (Eds.), *Learning-disabled/gifted children: Identification and programming* (pp. 117-139). Austin, TX: PRO-ED.

Gardner, H. (1999). *Intelligences reframed: Multiple intelligences.* New York, NY: Basic Books.

Glutting, J. J., McDermott, P. A., Prifitera, A., & McGrath, E. A. (1994). Core profile types for the WISC-III and WIAT: Their development and application in identifying multivariate IQ-achievement discrepancies. *School Psychology Review, 23,* 610-639.

Huberty, C. J., DiStefano, C., & Kamphaus, R. W. (1997). Behavioral clustering of school children. *Multivariate Behavioral Research, 32*(2), 105-134.

National Association for Gifted Children (NAGC). (1998). *Students with concomitant gifts and learning disabilities.* Washington, DC: Author.

Nielsen, M. E. (2002). Gifted students with learning disabilities: Recommendations for identification and programming. *Exceptionality, 10,* 93 111.

Norusis, M. J. (1995). *SPSS professional statistics 7.1.* Chicago, IL: SPSS, Inc.

Patchett, R. F., & Stansfield, M. (1992). Subtest scatter on the WISC-R with children of superior intelligence. *Psychology in the Schools, 29,* 5-10.

Prifitera, A., & Saklofske, D. H. (1998). *WISC-III clinical use and interpretation.* San Diego, CA: Academic Press.

Schiff, M. M., Kaufman, A. S., & Kaufman, N. L. (1981). Scatter analysis of WISC-R profiles for learning disabled children with superior intelligence. *Journal of Learning Disabilities, 14,* 400-404.

Seeley, K. R. (1998). Underachieving and talented learners with disabilities. In J. Van Tassel-Baska (Ed.), *Excellence in educating gifted and talented learners* (pp. 83-93). Denver, CO: Love Publishing.

Silver, S. J., & Clampit, M. K. (1990). WISC-R profiles of high ability children: Interpretation of verbal-performance discrepancies. *Gifted Children Quarterly, 34,* 76-79.

Silverman, L. K. (1998). Through the lens of giftedness. *Roeper Review, 20*(3), 204-210.

Silverman, L. K. (2003). Gifted children with learning disabilities. In N. A. Colangelo & G. A. Davis (Eds.), *Handbook of gifted education* (3rd ed., pp. 533-543). Boston, MA: Allyn & Bacon.

Starnes, W., Ginevan, J., Stokes, L., & Barton, J. (1988). *A study in the identification, differential diagnosis, and remediation of underachieving highly able students.* Paper presented at the annual meeting of the Council for Exceptional Children, Washington, DC.

The Psychological Corporation. (2002). *Wechsler Individual Achievement Test-Second Edition (WIAT-II).* San Antonio, TX: Author.

Ward, J. H., Jr. (1963). Hierarchical grouping to optimize an objective function. *American Statistical Association Journal, 58,* 236-244.

Wechsler, D. (1991). *Wechsler Intelligence Scale for Children- Third edition.* San

    Antonio, TX: Psychological Corporation.

Wechsler, D. (2003). *WISC-IV Technical and Interpretive Manual.* San Antonio, TX:

    Psychological Corporation.

Wilkinson, S. C. (1993). WISC-R profiles of children with superior intellectual ability.

    Gifted Child Quarterly, 37, 84-91.

APPENDIX B

CURRICULUM VITAE

LAURA B. McDONALD, M.A.

EDUCATION

2007 – Present
Azusa Pacific University
Department of Graduate Psychology
Azusa, CA (APA Accredited)
Student in Clinical Psychology with an emphasis in Family Psychology, PsyD program
PsyD in Clinical Psychology, Expected: August, 2011
Dissertation Topic: The Cognitive Ability of Twice-Exceptional Children and Adolescents.

2005 – 2007
Azusa Pacific University
Department of Graduate Psychology
Azusa, CA (WASC Accredited)
M.A. in Clinical Psychology with a Family Psychology emphasis (summa cum laude)

2002 – 2005
University of San Diego
College of Arts and Sciences
San Diego, CA
B.A. in Psychology (summa cum laude)

SUPERVISED CLINICAL EXPERIENCE

7/2010-06/30/2011
Predoctoral Clinical Psychology Internship
UCLA Semel Institute for Neuroscience and Human Behavior
Department of Psychiatry and Biobehavioral Sciences
David Geffen School of Medicine
760 Westwood Plaza
Los Angeles, CA 90095
(APA-Accredited)
Pediatric Neuropsychology Track (Meets requirements set forth by Division 40 [Neuropsychology] of the APA for specialty training in neuropsychology)
Advisor: Sandra Loo, Ph.D.

- *Setting*: A university teaching hospital.
- *Population*: Infants, children, adolescents, and young adults suffering from medical and more traditional child outpatient presenting problems. Diverse ethnic/racial, religious, and SES backgrounds.

- *Clientele Description*: Inpatients and outpatients referred by Neurology, Psychiatry, Organ Transplant, other medical clinics/units, and the community at large. Outpatient presenting problems commonly include ADHD, learning disorders, language disorders, pervasive developmental disorders and associated co-morbid psychiatric disorders. Medical problems typically include traumatic brain injury, epilepsy, organ transplants, genetic disorders, and cancer.
- *Responsibilities*: Perform comprehensive pediatric neuropsychological assessments (intake, testing, interpretation, report writing, feedback) for inpatients and outpatients through the Medical Psychology Assessment Center. Conduct comprehensive psychological assessments (intake, testing, interpretation, report writing, feedback) for infants and preschoolers through the Infant/Preschool Clinic. Conduct educational assessments for children and adolescents in inpatient and partial hospitalization programs. Co-lead PEERS social skills group for young adults with autism spectrum diagnoses. Participate in neurodiagnostic procedures including WADA testing, intra-operative brain mapping and brain cuttings. Conduct research relevant to cognitive and neurobiological functioning among children and adolescents with ADHD, Reading Disorder, and Autism. Administer neuropsychological test batteries as part of a COG autism research study.
- *Training*: Attend weekly didactic seminars in neuropsychology, functional neuroanatomy, developmental disabilities and psychopharmacology. Participate in weekly individual and group supervision.

8/2009- 6/2010   **Practicum V (Neuropsychological Assessment)**
Children's Hospital of Orange County
Department of Pediatric Psychology
455 South Main Street
Orange, CA 92868-3874
(714) 532 8481
Pediatric Neuropsychology Extern- Oncology Rotation
(Supervised hours: 820)
Supervisor: Marcos DiPinto, Ph.D.

- *Setting*: A pediatric psychology clinic within a children's hospital serving medically fragile children and adolescents.
- *Population*: Infants, children, adolescents, and young adults suffering from medical and more traditional child outpatient presenting problems.

- *Clientele Description*: Patients are typically affected by cancer, epilepsy, seizure disorders, prematurity, or traumatic brain injuries. Other more traditional outpatient presenting problems include learning disabilities, ADHD, pervasive developmental disorders, and emotional and behavioral difficulties. Diverse ethnic/racial, religious, and SES backgrounds.
- *Responsibilities*: Perform medical and educational record reviews, intake interviews, and comprehensive neuropsychological assessments with infants, children, adolescents and young adults (inpatient and outpatient). Administer, score, and interpret neuropsychological test batteries, compose comprehensive written reports, and provide feedback. Conduct neuropsychological test batteries as part of a COG research study. Consult with a multidisciplinary treatment team including pediatric neuropsychologists, pediatric neurologists, pediatric oncologists, and pediatric neuro-oncology surgeons. Attend bi-weekly tumor board meetings and neuro-onc grand rounds. Participate in Early Development Assessment Clinic (EDAC).
- *Training*: Attend weekly neuropsychology training seminars and presentations. Attend bi-weekly screen seminars. Participate in weekly individual and group supervision.

9/2008- 7/2009 **Practicum IV (Clinical)**
Verdugo Mental Health, Children Services
Glen Roberts Child Study Center
1514 E. Colorado Street
Glendale, CA 91205
(818) 244 7257
Practicum Student (Supervised hours: 1'055)
Supervisors: Mitesh Parekh, PsyD (individual supervisor); Karen Huestis, Ph.D. (group supervisor and training director)

- *Setting*: A nationally recognized community mental health clinic that treats children, adolescents, and families in a child-oriented setting.
- *Population*: Multiethnic children, adolescents, young adults and families of low socioeconomic status.
- *Clientele Description*: Clients suffer from issues related to trauma, depression, bipolar disorder, autism, anxiety, ADHD, learning disability, and substance abuse. Diverse ethnic/racial and religious backgrounds and low SES.

- *Responsibilities*: Provided individual and family psychotherapy and play therapy. Completed psychodiagnostic assessment batteries; co-lead a weekly therapeutic group for adolescents, and provided parent education.
- *Training*: Attended twice-weekly trainings, case conferences, and seminars. Participated in weekly individual and group supervision.

12/2007- 07/2009   **Practicum III (Neuropsychological Assessment)**
Pediatric Neurodevelopment Institute
Azusa Pacific University
918 E. Alosta
Azusa, CA 91702
(626)-815-5421
Senior Assessment Clerk (Supervised hours: 550)
Supervisors: Janiece Turnbull, Ph.D.; Beth Houskamp, Ph.D.; Annette Ermshar, Ph.D., ABPP

- *Setting*: A university-based, multidisciplinary diagnostic, treatment, and research center for children and adolescents.
- *Population*: Children, adolescents, and young adults.
- *Clientele Description*: Patients present with learning disabilities, ADHD, pervasive developmental disorders, language disorders, emotional and behavioral difficulties, as well as giftedness.
- *Responsibilities*: Conducted comprehensive neuropsychological assessments with children, adolescents and young adults. Administered, scored, and interpreted neuropsychological test batteries and composed comprehensive written reports. Consulted with a multidisciplinary treatment team including pediatric neuropsychologists, school psychologists, speech and language pathologists, pediatric physical therapists, and pediatric nurses.
- *Training*: Attended weekly trainings, and treatment team meetings. Participated in weekly group and individual supervision meetings.

8/2007- 8/2008   **Practicum II (Assessment)**
Hathaway-Sycamores
Child and Family Services
625 Fair Oaks Avenue, Suite 300
South Pasadena, CA 91030
(626) 395-7100
Assessment Clerk (Supervised hours: 757)

Supervisors: Rochelle Lee, PsyD; Delany Thrasher, Ph.D.

- *Setting*: Comprehensive outpatient treatment program.
- *Population*: Children, adolescents and young adults.
- *Clientele Description*: Seriously emotionally disturbed children and adolescents from residential treatment facilities (RCL-14), outpatient settings, and non-public school programs; young adults in transitional living programs, and children in foster care. Diverse ethnic/racial, religious, and SES backgrounds. Variety of diagnostic categories: mood disorders, anxiety disorders, psychotic disorders, pervasive developmental disorders, disruptive behavioral disorders, post-traumatic stress disorders, learning disorders, and mental retardation.
- *Responsibilities*: Conducted record review, intake interviews, as well as cognitive, achievement, personality, and projective assessments. Administered, scored, and interpreted psychometric tests and composed comprehensive written reports. Provided differential diagnosis, treatment recommendations, and feedback to treatment team and family. Consulted with a multidisciplinary treatment team, including psychiatrists, therapists, social workers, educators, and residential staff to assist with treatment planning.
- *Training*: Attended weekly training seminars and group supervision on topics including psychodiagnostic assessment and interpretation, wraparound services, residential services, and childhood and adolescent development. Received weekly individual supervision.

09/2006 – 06/2007 **Practicum I (Clinical)**
Child and Family Development Center
Azusa Pacific University
918 E. Alosta
Azusa, CA 91702
(626)-815-5421
Practicum Student (Supervised hours: 470)
Supervisors: David Brokaw, Ph.D.; Robin Huff-Musgrove, Ph.D.

- *Setting*: A community-based counseling facility in a low SES community offering individual, marriage, and family therapy services with fees based on a sliding scale.
- *Population*: Children, adolescents, college students, adults, and families.
- *Clientele Description*: Clients from an ethnically diverse community presenting with issues related to ADHD, mood

disorders, anxiety disorders, adjustment disorders, body image concerns, trauma, parenting issues, and relationship problems.
- *Responsibilities*: Provided individual therapy to children, adolescents, college students, and adults.
- *Training*: Attended weekly staff development and training seminars. Received weekly individual and group supervision.

Valleydale Elementary School
Azusa Unified School District
700 South Lark Ellen
Azusa, CA 91702
Supervisor: David Brokaw, Ph.D.

- *Setting*: Elementary school in a low-income community.
- *Population*: Ethnically diverse elementary aged children and their families.
- *Clientele Description*: Children with emotional, interpersonal, and behavioral problems. Issues addressed include grief, trauma, divorce, family conflict, anxiety, depression, and anger management.
- *Responsibilities*: Provided therapy to elementary school students and their families, focused primarily on low SES and minority populations.
- *Training*: Attended weekly staff development and training seminars. Received weekly individual and group supervision.

01/06-05/06   **Pre-Practicum (Clinical)**
Child and Family Development Center
Azusa Pacific University
918 E. Alosta
Azusa CA 91702
(626)-815-5412
Practicum Student (Supervised hours: 30)
Supervisor: Sheryn T. Scott, Ph.D.

- *Setting*: Community counseling center in low SES community.
- *Population:* Undergraduate college students.
- *Clientele Description*: Young adults suffering from a variety of mental health issues including relationship problems, substance abuse issues, eating disorders, spiritual concerns and adjustment disorders.
- *Responsibilities:* Provided individual psychotherapy.

SUPERVISED WORK EXPERIENCE

03/2009- 06/2010 **Neurobehavior Services, Inc.**
685 E. California Blvd
Pasadena, CA 91106
Assessment Clerk (10 hours/week)
Supervisor: Janiece Turnbull, Ph.D.

- *Setting*: Private practice providing neuropsychological assessments and consultation for children and adolescents.
- *Population*: Children and adolescents.
- *Clientele Description*: Clients from an ethnically diverse community presenting with learning disabilities, language disorders, ADHD, mood disorders, anxiety disorders, pervasive developmental disorders, and disruptive behavior disorders.
- *Responsibilities*: Administer, score, and interpret neuropsychological test batteries and compose comprehensive written reports.

ADDITIONAL SUPERVISED CLINICAL EXPERIENCE

08/2004-12/2004 **The Salk Institute for Biological Studies**
Laboratory for Cognitive Neuroscience
La Jolla, CA
Practicum Student (15 hours/week)
Supervisors: Teresa Doyle, Ph.D.; Ursula Bellugi, Ph.D.

- *Project Title*: The MacArthur Communicative Development Inventory for Children with Downs and Williams Syndrome.
- *Setting*: Premier independent, non-profit, scientific research institute.
- *Population*: Young children.
- *Clientele Description*: Young children suffering from Downs or Williams Syndrome.
- *Responsbilities:* Worked on research project comparing the language development in children with Downs and Williams Syndrome as part of a study investigating critical brain regions involved, and clues to the genetic pathways underlying, affiliative social behavior. Duties included data analysis using StatView, as well as preparation and presentation of findings. Attended training seminars and staff development. Received weekly individual supervision.

08/2004-12/2004   **Southern Sudanese Community Center**
San Diego, CA
Practicum Student (8 hours/week)
Supervisor: Dep Tuany.

- *Setting*: Non-profit community center assisting Sudanese refugees in their resettlement through education, social, economic, and cultural support.
- *Population*: Children, adolescents and their families.
- *Clientele Description*: Southern Sudanese refugees who have been forced to leave their country because of ongoing religious, ethnic and political persecution.
- *Responsibilities*: Mentored and tutored newly immigrated Southern Sudanese children and adolescents in Math, Reading, and English, as well as provided support to parents. Received weekly individual and group supervision.

01/2004-06/2004   **Head Start**
San Diego, CA
Practicum Student (10 hours/week)
Supervisor: Julie Garrett.

- *Setting:* Federally funded early childhood education program.
- *Population:* Children ages 3-5 years old.
- *Clientele Description:* Preschool children from low-income families.
- *Responsibilities:* Supervised children, trained children in writing and spelling, and participated in group activities related to children's interest. Met with parents to discuss children's development. Received weekly individual supervision.

08/2003-12/2003   **Children's Hospital San Diego**
Child and Adolescent Services Research Center
San Diego, CA
Practicum Student (10 hours/week)
Supervisor: Hazel Atuel, M.A. and Virginia Renker, MPH

- *Project title*: Safe Schools/Healthy Students.
- *Setting:* Children's Hospital.
- *Population:* Adolescents and their parents/caregivers.
- *Clientele Description:* Adolescents receiving violence prevention education.
- *Responsibilities:* Conducted telephone interviews with adolescents and their parents participating in a study

investigating violence prevention education. Data collection and data entry. Received weekly supervision.

PUBLICATIONS

McDonald, L., Welsh, R., Houskamp, B., & Jiang, Y. H. (in press). The factor structure of the short sensory profile with a Latino preschool population. *Assessment.*

Hirayama, K., Fok, A., **McDonald, L.**, Wolff, M., Houskamp, B.M., Radisavljevic, K., Fok, J, Racaza, R., Diener, R. (in press). The Relationship between externalizing behaviors, attention and executive functioning in explosive children. *The Clinical Neuropsychologist.*

McDonald, L., Semon, K., & Do, A. (in press). Attitudes toward marriage in Switzerland and the United States. *Journal of Psychological Inquiry.*

Houskamp, B. M., Scott, S. T., Neumann, D. A., & **McDonald, L.** (2010). Assessing and treating battered women. In M. Paludi & F. A. Denmark (Eds). *Victims of sexual assault and abuse: Resources and responses for individuals and families Volume II: Cultural, community, educational and advocacy responses.* New York: Praeger.

Gunn, T. E., Tavegia, B. D., Houskamp, B. M., **McDonald, L. B.**, Bustrum, J. M., Welsh, R. K., & Mok, D. S. (2009). Relationship between sensory deficits and externalizing behaviors in an urban, Latino preschool population. *Journal of Child and Family Studies, 18(6)* 653-661.

Houskamp, B. M., Radisavljevic, K., & **McDonald, L.** (2008). Using collaborative problem solving to address developmental delays in gifted children. *The 2e Newsletter, 31*, 14-18.

MANUSCRIPTS IN SUBMISSION

Tavegia, B., Houskamp, B., **McDonald, L.**, & Holler, R. (Under Review). *Sensory deficits and their relationship to pervasive developmental disorders in an urban preschool population.*

MANUSCRIPTS IN PREPARATION

McDonald, L., Houskamp, B., Welsh, R., Scott, S. & Beljan, P. (Under Review). *The cognitive ability patterns of twice-exceptional children and adolescents.*

Radisavljevic, K., Houskamp, B., **McDonald, L.**, & Beljan, P. (Under Review). Exploring ADHD in a population of gifted children: An examination into the role of executive functioning.

McDonald, L., Loo, S., Humphrey, L., & McCracken, J. (in preparation). Working memory and behavioral inhibition deficits in children with ADHD and Reading Disorder.

Di Pinto, M., Shen, V., **McDonald, L.,** Mucci, G., & Schenk, J. (in preparation). Intellectual outcome in bilingual and monolingual children with medulloblastoma.

Di Pinto, M., Shen, V., **McDonald, L.,** Mucci, G., & Schenk, J. (in preparation). Neurocognitive late effect in bilingual and monolingual children with acute lymphoblastic leukemia.

PROFESSIONAL PRESENTATIONS

Houskamp, B., **McDonald, L.,** & Racaza, R. (October 2010). *The neuropychological processing of twice-exceptional children.* Workshop presentation for the New England Conference on Gifted & Talented Education in Partnership with SENG and AEGUS, Hartford, Connecticut.

Di Pinto, M., Shen, V., **McDonald, L.,** Mucci, G., Schenk, J., Templeman, T., Pathare, J., Hawking, K., & Begino, C. (June 2010). Intellectual outcome in bilingual and monolingual children with medulloblastoma. Paper presented at the International Symposium on Pediatric Neuro-Oncology. Vienna, Austria.

McDonald, L., Houskamp, B., Radisavljevic, K., Mota, E., Offinga, T., & Beljan, P. (August 2009). *The cognitive profile of twice-exceptional children.* Poster presentation for the American Psychological Association Annual Convention, Toronto, ON.

Radisavljevic, K., **McDonald, L.,** Houskamp, B., Mota, E., Offinga, T., & Beljan, P. (August 2009). *Attention and executive functioning in a population of gifted children.* Poster presentation for the American Psychological Association Annual Convention, Toronto, ON.

Hirayama, K., Fok, A., **McDonald, L.,** Wolff, M., Houskamp, B.M., Radisavljevic, K., Fok, J, Racaza, R., Diener, R. (August 2009). *The Relationship between externalizing behaviors, attention and executive functioning in explosive children.* Poster presentation for the American Psychological Association Annual Convention, Toronto, ON.

Houskamp, B. M., Fok, A., **McDonald, L.,** & Radisavljevic, K. (July 2008). *An exploration of the relationships between sensory processing, information processing, attention, affect and behavior regulation in twice exceptional children: A theoretical overview, initial pilot data and recommendations for parents and teachers.* Workshop presented at the Supporting Emotional Needs of the Gifted, Annual Conference, Salt Lake City, Utah.

McDonald, L., Houskamp, B., Gunn, T., Radisavljevic, K., & McIllnay, J. (August 2007). *The relationship between sensory deficits, ADHD, and ODD among Guatemalan school-age children.* Poster presented at the Annual Convention of the American Psychological Association, San Francisco, California.

McDonald, L., Welsh, R., Houskamp, B., Jiang, Y.H., & Tulleners Lesh, A. (November 2006). *The factor structure of the short sensory profile with a Latino preschool population.* Poster presented at the Queen Elizabeth Centre's Early Childhood Conference, University of Melbourne, Melbourne, Australia.

McDonald, L., & Lento, J. (May 2005). *Gender differences in perceived sociocultural pressure to be thin.* Poster presented at the Student Research & Internship Conference, University of San Diego.

McDonald, L., Semon, K., & Do, A. (April 2005). *Attitudes toward marriage in Switzerland and the United States.* Poster presented at the Western Psychological Association Conference, Portland, Oregon.

McDonald, L., & Lento, J. (April 2005). *Gender differences in perceived sociocultural pressure to be thin.* Poster presented at the Western Psychological Association Conference, Portland, Oregon.

McDonald, L., Semon, K., & Do, A. (October 2004). *Attitudes toward marriage in Switzerland and the United States.* Paper presented at the Psychology Research Colloquium, University of San Diego.

McDonald, L., Semon, K., & Do, A. (May 2004). *Attitudes toward marriage in Switzerland and the United States.* Poster presented at the Student Research & Internship Conference, University of San Diego.

GRANTS SUBMITTED

Martin, L., Wolff, M., Houskamp, B., **McDonald, L.**, Connolly, M. (February 2009). Evaluation of the efficacy of neurofeedback therapy on executive function in children with autism. *Autism Speaks.*

Martin, L., Wolff, M., Houskamp, B., **McDonald, L.**, Fok, A., & Legardy, S. (June 2009). The efficacy of neurofeedback therapy on executive function in children with autism. *NIMH & NIH.*

HONORS AND AWARDS

2010	**Alpha Chi, National College Honor Scholarship Society,** Azusa Pacific University
2008	**Research Travel Grant,** Azusa Pacific University

2007	**Research Travel Grant**, Azusa Pacific University
2005	**First Prize in the Psi Chi/J. P. Guilford Undergraduate Research Award**, American Psychological Association, Psi Chi
2005	**Distinguished Graduate in Psychology Award**, University of San Diego
2005	**Departmental Honors Award in Psychology**, University of San Diego
2005	**Highest Academic Average Award**, University of San Diego
2005	**Phi Beta Kappa**, University of San Diego
2005	**Kappa Gamma Pi**, University of San Diego
2004	**Highest Academic Average Award**, University of San Diego
2004	**Associated Students Academic Research Grant**, University of San Diego
2003-2005	**Dean's List, First Honors**, University of San Diego

RESEARCH EXPERIENCE

2006 – 2010
Dissertation topic: The Cognitive Ability of Twice-Exceptional Children and Adolescents
Dissertation Chair: Beth Houskamp, Ph.D.
Committee: Robert K. Welsh, Ph.D., ABPP; Sheryn Scott, Ph.D.
Dissertation Proposal Approved: 2-26-2009
Dissertation Colloquium Approved: 9-16-2009
Dissertation Defense Approved: 6-30-2010

2010- Present
University of California, Los Angeles
Research Assistant
Administer neuropsychological battery to participants in an autism COG research study. Participate in research project, which is part of a multisite autism research grant. Duties include researching and selecting neuropsychological measures best suited for the study, training investigators from participating sites in the administration of the instruments, collecting results, and preparing projects. Developing independent research projects in the area of ADHD and reading disorder. Preparing results for presentation and publication.

2009- Present
Children's Hospital of Orange County
Research Assistant
Conduct research with neuro-oncology team investigating the neurocognitive outcome of bilingual children and adolescents with a history of medulloblastoma or acute lymphoblastic leukemia (ALL). Participate in ALL COG research study. Administer and score neuropsychological batteries. Enter data and analyze

findings. Present results at international conference and prepare study for publication.

2006 – Present	**Azusa Pacific University** **Department of Graduate Psychology** *Research Assistant* Assist faculty with research projects, including literature reviews, data entry, data analysis, and article writing. *Supervisor*: Beth Houskamp, Ph.D.
2005 – Present	**Azusa Pacific University** *Member of Research Group* Member of an interdisciplinary research group investigating neurodevelopmental disabilities and information processing in children and adolescents. Duties include data collection, data entry and analysis using SPSS, project preparation and presentation.
2004 – 2005	**University of San Diego** *Research Assistant* *Project Title:* Gender Differences in Perceived Sociocultural Pressure to be Thin. Duties included literature review, hypothesis construction, project preparation and presentation. *Supervisor*: Jennifer Lento, Ph.D.

TEACHING EXPERIENCE

Fall, 2008	**Azusa Pacific University** **Department of Graduate Psychology** *Teaching Assistant* for Robert Welsh, Ph.D., ABPP, Research Design Duties included designing and teaching a weekly one-hour SPSS lab covering univariate and multivariate statistics; graded weekly homework assignments.
Spring, 2008	**Azusa Pacific University** **Department of Undergraduate Psychology** *Teaching Assistant* for Loren Martin, Ph.D, Research Methods Duties included maintaining office hours to grade research papers and schedule regular meetings with students to provide feedback regarding the design of their research projects and the quality of their APA-style research papers.
Fall, 2003	**University of San Diego** **Department of Foreign Languages and Literatures** *Apprentice Teacher* for Christiane Staninger, Ph.D., German I

Responsibilities included teaching a German I Drill class three hours per week, preparing lessons, and preparing a presentation with the students.

SUPERVISION EXPERIENCE

Fall, 2008 **Azusa Pacific University**
Department of Graduate Psychology
Duties: Supervised two first year doctoral students conducting individual psychotherapy. Supervision involved a weekly review of students' video or audio taped sessions, feedback regarding progress of therapy, role-plays, and short lectures related to theoretical and practical applications of clinical therapy.
Setting: Supervision Course
Professor: Sheryn Scott, Ph.D.

OTHER PROFESSIONAL ACTIVITIES

2008- Present **Assistant Reviewer**, *Women's Health Issues*

2007- 2010 **Committee Member**, American Psychological Association, Division 43 Family Psychology

2004-2005 **Secretary**, Psi Chi (National Honor Society in Psychology)

PROFESSIONAL AFFILIATIONS

Graduate Student Affiliate, American Psychological Association

Graduate Student Affiliate, American Psychological Association, Division 40 Clinical Neuropsychology

Graduate Student Affiliate, International Neuropsychological Society

Graduate Student Affiliate, American Psychological Association, Division 43 Family Psychology

HONOR SOCIETIES

Member of Alpha Chi (National College Honor Scholarship Society)

Member of Phi Beta Kappa (National Honor Society)

Member of Kappa Gamma Pi (National Catholic Graduate Honor Society)

Member of Psi Chi (National Honor Society in Psychology)

CERTIFICATES

CPR and Standard First Aid-Adult, Child and Infant (December 2008)
EMS Safety Services

Professional Assault Crisis Training (Pro-ACT), Zero-Restraint Training (August 2007)
Hathaway-Sycamores Child and Family Services

Human Participant Protection Certification, National Institutes of Health (August 2007)
Hathaway-Sycamores Child and Family Services

Child Abuse Training Seminar (January 2006)
Azusa Pacific University

LANGUAGES

Fluent in English, German, and French

CPSIA information can be obtained at www.ICGtesting.com
Printed in the USA
BVOW08s1545161213

339281BV00011B/699/P